CONTENTS

Why I wrote this book	1
Awareness Building	10
Foundational Marketing	20
Follow-Up System	31
Post-Sale Retention and Engagement	38
Awareness Building	45
Advanced Marketing Ideas	71
Joint Marketing	94
Foundational Marketing Action Plan	109
Online Product Seller Sample Strategy	119
High Price Point	122
Loyalty Program/Credibility Boosters	125

Devin James Kerns

WHY I WROTE THIS BOOK

"The best product doesn't always win; often, it just comes down to who is better at marketing." This seemingly casual remark I heard from an entrepreneur completely changed my business paradigm and led to the writing of this book. Why was this seemingly unremarkable comment so, well, remarkable? The reason is, if it's true, someone could launch a product superior in every way to anything in its class and still be beaten spectacularly by an inferior product due to the inferior product's marketing skills!

Some might be skeptical about this, but anyone who has been in business for a while knows this is true. In fact, in my own personal career, I've actually managed to take objectively worse products and services and out-promote some far better products simply by using better promotional strategies.

The implications of this are staggering. Marketing is not some afterthought once you create your product or service. In most cases, it's equally as important as the product/service itself, and in some cases, it's actually more important than the actual item being sold (think luxury goods).

So here is an unfortunate truth: Not only do entrepreneurs need to have a great product or service but they also need to be (or have on their team) world-class marketers in order to succeed.

I realize that this is a tall order for many businesses, and that is the reason I wrote this book. I want to not only level the playing field but give readers a huge advantage over their competition.

Why This Book?

So as we've established, marketing is rather important, but there are hundreds of marketing books out there to choose from. Why is this one unique and what makes it worth reading? Well, most marketing books fall into one of two categories. They typically are either filled with a high-level vague strategy that is hard to implement, or they are just a laundry list of marketing ideas with no strategy or cohesion.

In terms of cooking, the first is a list of instructions with no ingredients. The second gives you a bunch of ingredients but no instructions. In either event, I'm not coming over for dinner!

This book is my attempt to put everything together for you: the ingredients and the instructions. We are going to start with some fundamental marketing strategies and concepts, and while I readily admit that they are not particularly revolutionary, they will inform the fundamental "why" behind the marketing tactics that we cover after.

These marketing tactics in turn, will, again, start out as foundational, but they will quickly become some advanced tactics that you've likely never heard of before. For those that have been in the marketing game for a while, you will likely enjoy this section the most, as I'll pull back the curtain and share some hard-hitting, highly effective marketing tactics.

However, as stated earlier, the goal of this book was not to simply throw some neat marketing ideas out there but to give a complete marketing system that a business can copy and modify based on their needs. For example, you'll find different tactics that you can use independently, but also how you can integrate them together - such as how you can take something as old school as postcards and make them cutting-edge by integrating them with digital marketing. You'll likely have some fun here thinking up new ways to synthesize both offline and online tactics to maximize your marketing bang.

Finally, you'll get a couple of complete step-by-step action lists that you can start implementing immediately based on your business type. From here, feel free to cut what you don't want or add what you do. The goal was to create a robust, yet flexible framework for you to build your marketing plan off of. By the end, you should have a detailed, complete, and powerful plan to jumpstart your new venture or breathe some new life into your established one.

Surprise Bonus

As I was finalizing the book, I realized I wanted to take it one step further. While writing about a topic or how to do something specific like setting a website is fine, the power of seeing it done right in front of you cannot be overstated. That is why, for those who have purchased the book like yourself, I'm including step by step video tutorials and a variety of key topics. Some of those topics include, recruiting affiliates, Facebook advertising, social marketing, lead generation, funnel building, website building and more! To access the tutorials, simply visit jumpstartmarketing/resources.

One last thing: If you have any feedback on the book, catch an error, or want to grab a coffee (For my Bay Area readers), please email me at Devin@jumpstartmarketing.org

Why Do People Buy?

Good marketing starts with good questions, so let's start with the absolute, most basic question - why do people buy? If we know why people buy, we can then figure out how to get them to buy. That will, in turn, inform our marketing strategy.

At the most basic level, I will argue that people buy because of three key factors. The first is an awareness that the product or service exists. Second, people must have a need or desire for which the product/service offers a solution. Lastly, people will buy the product they expect to get the most overall benefit from if competition exists. Astute readers may realize that I am downplaying the factor of price, but we'll talk about that separately.

For now though, let's run through a quick example to make this more concrete: Let's say you are feeling hungry. In other words, you have a need that you would like to meet. Second, you look at nearby restaurants. That is, you are becoming aware of what restaurants exist in the area. Finally, you choose a restaurant based on what restaurant you expect to receive the biggest benefit from. Perhaps, to do this, you look at Yelp to see the reviews and look at their menus to compare prices. Ultimately, you decide on the one that received good reviews and is moderately priced. Again, you do this in order to determine which restaurant you expect to provide you with the maximum benefit.

As you can see, in order for people to make

any buying decision at all, they must, at the very least, have a perceived need/desire for the product as well as an awareness that it exists to satisfy the desire. Typically, though, as a business facing competition, you must make your prospects believe they will receive the largest overall benefit from using your product or service. Let's now break down each one of these factors in depth and see how it can inform our marketing strategy.

Who needs what you got?

Since buying decisions typically start with a need or desire to solve a particular problem, it makes sense then to examine the type of person who might need or want to the product or service you offer. After all, they are going to be the most likely type of people to buy after becoming aware of your offering.

Most businesses already know the type of people they want to go after, so I'll keep this short. However, if you haven't thought about it before, really consider who can benefit most from your offering and what their characteristics are. Do they share a particular geographical location or are they high earners from across the country? Knowing the demographics of your target audience informs not only the medium in which you market but also the message itself.

Beyond your typical demographic information, some businesses wisely look for events in people's lives that prompt them to become potential customers. Many times, knowing these events is more powerful than any demographic information.

One great example of this can be found in real estate. Most people in the course of their lives buy and sell real estate, thereby making almost everyone a potential customer. Unfortunately, this poses a big problem for real estate agents trying to find new clients since targeting everyone always a losing strategy. Instead, it's much wiser (and profitable) to look for events in the lives of people that cause them to buy and sell real estate. For example, many couples who get divorced will sell their homes. Similarly, many times a newlywed couple will buy a house together. While the information may be a bit tricky to obtain, having it will greatly narrow the field of prospective clients.

As many marketers know, finding these events can be tricky and mistakes can prove to be very expensive. Consider a high-end restaurant owner that mistakenly assumes her event is people becoming hungry. While this may be true for some places like fast food restaurants where people just wander in when they are hungry, for restaurants that are reservation-driven, it's not likely the case. This is evidenced by the fact that people make reservations weeks in advance when they are very much not hungry!

Instead, the primary binding event is the decision to go out for a date night or an outing with family, which then necessitates the "Where should we eat" question. While perhaps, a bit nuanced, it is important to understand the distinction, as it will drastically change the marketing message and the target of the message. The former might push the message of cheap yummy food targeting say, single parents who come home after a long day at work. The later, however, might focus on selling an experience to married professionals.

Now that we've covered who you should be targeting based on how likely they will respond to your offer, the next question to answer is how do you make them aware of your product or service? Most of the book is dedicated to answering that question since often times that is the largest hurdle you will face.

AWARENESS BUILDING

When is the last time you bought something you had never heard of before? The answer by definition must be never. It's impossible to buy something without hearing about it somewhere first, even if it's at the last second.

The goal of awareness building is to simultaneously associate your brand with the broader industry you are in and build up the expected benefit in the minds of your prospects, which we will cover next. For example, Joe's Auto Repair Shop wants to get people to associate his brand with the broader category of auto repair so that when their car breaks down, they will think about his shop. But more than just that, he wants to convince them that his shop is better than all the others because, odds are, the prospects can think of at least one other shop that they can go to.

It's important to keep in mind that hearing about something one time is usually not enough; people must have enough interactions with your brand to get it to stick. In most cases, your prospect isn't going to be ready to buy your offering at the exact second your marketing message hits him or her. Therefore, it's extremely important to build up these interactions over time (often with automated follow-up). So when they do decide to buy, you'll be one of the first they think about. We'll cover this topic extensively in our follow-up chapter. For now, let's dive in to how you can build that awareness in a way that allows you to win the hearts of your potential customers and beat out the competition.

Beating the Competition

It's worth noting that in the absence of competition, all you really need is that awareness that your product or service exists. If I want my car fixed and only one repair shop around me exists (that I know of), guess which one I am going to? Unfortunately, as stated, in all likelihood, prospects know at least one of your competitors.

So in the presence of this competition, where the potential customer is aware of said competition, what is the deciding factor? Let's examine competition in the form of a very relatable example - deciding which movie to see.

To set this up, let's start with the problem or desire, which, in this case, is usually the desire to be entertained. Now assuming the prospective moviegoers are aware that two movies are playing in the theater, which is usually the case, they will instinctively consider which movie they think will be "better" or more entertaining. In other words, they ***expect*** one movie to be more entertaining than the other and, therefore, they typically choose that movie over the other. More broadly, people select the business that they expect to fulfill the desire most fully or solve their problem most successfully. For example, I *expected Star Wars* to be more entertaining than the new *Jumanji,* so I went and saw the former.

The first key point here is: All things being equal, people will use the product or service they expect the most benefit out of. Why not choose a Tesla over Civic if the price is the same? We expect the Tesla to be a better car than Civic, so we would be naturally drawn to the former.

Now the really interesting thing, going back to our movie example, is that my expectations didn't line up with reality. In my opinion, *Jumanji* was a far more entertaining movie, yet *The Last Jedi* got my money. For better or worse, when it comes to marketing, perception is everything. Unless a prospective customer has personal experience with your goods, all they can do is expect a benefit from it. They won't really know until they buy. Therefore, fundamentally, the product with the highest expectations wins. The trick then is to find what benefit or value people seek to derive from your product or service and then do everything in your power to reinforce that perception so that when it comes time to make the purchasing decision, they expect your offering to be superior in the areas they care about most.

The starting question then to ask yourself is why do people use your product or service? You probably know who buys, but why do they buy? Many times, it's not as obvious as you may think. It may be for convenience; it could be for the price. People usually refer to this as your unique selling proposition. What benefit do you give to your customers that is unique to your business?

Here's a funny example. I don't think Starbucks coffee is all that wonderful. In fact, today's brew, which I'm presently drinking, is particularly bad. In spite of this, I come here maybe 2-3 times a week and am a gold member. Why? Because they offer a fantastic environment to lounge, meet with people, or get work done. The primary benefit they give me is the environment. Of course, not everyone shares my view on that. Many people go to Starbucks to grab their morning coffee and then drive to work. They don't care about the environment; they care about their coffee. From a strategic perspective, Starbucks should probably focus on this grab-and-go crowd since they are more profitable, but that's a discussion for another time.

The main point I'm making is that people will choose your product or service over another when the total expected benefit of using your offering outweighs the competition. That total expected benefit is a combination of the benefit they care about most, the price, and their belief in your ability to provide it. While we have talked a fair bit about the expected benefit, let's discuss how price plays into this value equation.

The Role of Price

Earlier, I asked, all things being equal, would you take a Civic or a Tesla. Most people would say Tesla, yet most saying that would be more likely to actually own a Civic. Clearly, something else is at play here. That thing is price.

Let's go back to our movie example. If you expect both movies to be equally entertaining but movie A is 50% cheaper for whatever reason, you probably will go see it instead of movie B. That situation is pretty easy, but what if you expect movie B to be better but movie A is 50% cheaper? What will you do then? It probably depends. It likely will depend on how much better you expect movie B to be. If you expect movie B to be far better than movie A, you will probably pay the full price to see movie B. However, if you think it will only be somewhat better, then that's where things get interesting.

Some people may choose the discount and save money, while others will choose to spend more, expecting to get more entertainment. Typically, people with more money will be happy to spend more to get a larger benefit, whereas people with less will likely forgo some benefit to save some money. While this is just a generalization, it is good to keep this in mind.

The point of this little behavioral economics lesson is that people will buy on a combination of expected benefit and price, which we will call value. Though just as before, it's *expected* value, not delivered value. With this in mind, companies will typically either offer a low price, low benefit product, a middle of the road approach, or a high price, high benefit product. This allows for the targeting of different segments of the market. Since the perception of value will differ from customer to customer, the different combinations of benefit and price may be well received from one market segment but not by others. Therefore, it's important to determine not only what your customers care about, but also what pricing and messaging strategy you wish to employ.

Gap has done this astoundingly well. They target the low end of the market with their Old Navy brand. Gap itself targets mid-market, and Banana Republic targets the high end. You'll often see their stores sitting side by side each other in order to leverage supply chain efficiencies, but since they target such different markets, none of the stores cannibalize the others.

Who you going to target based on demographics and/or shared events, what do they care about, and your price point.

Marketing Message

We will now use everything we have discussed so far to create a simple, focused messaged. Start by recalling who are you are targeting based on demographics and/or shared events. Next, consider what these people care about/why they would want to buy from you. Next, take a look at your competition and see what value combinations they are offering. If they are targeting high end, consider going after mid-market or lower. If most of them are going low, go high.

The key here is, if at all possible, to target the segments that are currently underserved. It's easier to create a monopoly in one segment of the market than to fight to carve out market share in an existing segment that is already being served well. Once you decide which segment to target, you'll want to craft your message accordingly. If you are targeting the high end of the market, focus on pushing the expected benefit hard. Avoid talking about price and simply focus on how superior your solution is to everything on the market. For targeting the lower end, it's the opposite. For the middle, it's going to be equal parts price and benefits offered.

No matter which approach you end up taking, never lose sight of pushing the most important benefit that your product or service provides. This will be your core message that you will use constantly in your marketing pieces.

Perception Channels

Now that we have covered why people buy and you have a good starting point for your core messaging, let's lastly cover how perception is created and reinforced. It's important to understand how these opinions and expectations are informed because our marketing strategy will take advantage of these different channels to promote that core message we just discussed. Broadly, those three channels by which perception is formed are: what the company says, what other people say, and past experiences.

Company set expectations: Any commercial or marketing piece is a direct attempt to influence the prospect. Usually, they try to influence the perceived value of their products to the customers. Since the message is coming from the company itself, consumers will put less weight in it than the other two sources. Also, it's important to note that some companies have a reputation for being more or less honest than others and that will also affect how the message is received.

Past Experiences: Let's say you've bought three Toyotas in a row and each and every one of them broke down at 50k miles. Let's further say that you are planning on buying a new car and that you, as a consumer, value reliability. As you browse for new cars, you see a Toyota commercial touting the reliability of the car you've purchased three times. Would this commercial change your perception toward the reliability of Toyotas? No, it'd probably just make you laugh.

These types of past experiences create lasting beliefs and perceptions for brands that aren't easy to change. This is why good customer service is so important and should be consider a marketing function. Many of even the most loyal customers are just one bad experience away from switching brands and no amount of subsequent advertising will matter.

Other People – When we lack personal experience of a product or service, we typically seek out other people who have had a personal experience with it. For example, you probably read the reviews for this book before buying it. If they were bad, you probably wouldn't have bought it. Testimonials, experiences of friends, critic reviews, and product reviews all fall under this social proof category. For this reason, it is important to have a solid review strategy which we will cover later.

Putting the Strategy Together

We've covered a fair bit of theory at this point, and now it is time to translate it to an actionable marketing plan using what we have covered so far as a foundation. First, Second, we need to identify the people who will benefit the most from that value. Second, we established that we need to know the value (key benefit + price position) that we are delivering. Third, we must craft the marketing message in a way that communicates that value proposition in a way that resonates with our prospects. Finally, we need a way (or multiple ways) to continually communicate that value message through the channels we discussed earlier with the dual goals of building awareness and strengthening that value proposition.

From here on, we are going to be focusing on that final bit. How can we best use those three channels to communicate our marketing message? Particularly, though, since we have the most control over the company's messaging channel, it will be the focal point of our marketing pipeline.

A typical pipeline, then, that combines everything we have discussed so far in an efficient and cost-effective system may look something like this.

> Customer Acquisition Channel → Website → Info Capture → Follow Up → Sale → Social Proof → Referrals

While your particular marketing pipeline might look different, this is a good starting point and can be adjusted as needed. First we need to start with a customer acquisition channel or channels (PPC, Direct Mail, etc.) that will serve as our initial awareness/influence building campaign. We then need a follow-up system that allows us to maintain that awareness in a cost-effective manner. One way to do that is through lead capture via a website and then follow up via email as shown above. Finally, post-sale, we will ensure that the customer has had a good experience and also develop a customer retention and social proof plan to keep the customers we've got and strengthen our perceived value to new customers.

FOUNDATIONAL MARKETING

Congratulations, we are officially done with theory! Let's now turn our focus and get started on the fun stuff - implementing the strategy. Often times, business owners and startups want to jump straight away into awareness and influence building, which is the sexy stuff like Facebook ads and YouTube videos, but as a result, they fail to build a robust marketing foundation. Without that proper foundation to capture and nurture leads, they end up spending thousands without much of anything to show for it. I myself was guilty of this when I first started my marketing career. I pushed expensive traffic to my websites and if the prospect didn't instantly buy, which accounts for about 80% of all traffic, I was out of luck.

To reiterate that, one well-known marketer once told me, "People don't have traffic problems; they have conversion problems. After all, you can always buy more traffic." I think he is right on the money. If your marketing foundation is strong, that is, your conversion efforts and follow-up system, you can always turn on the traffic nozzle to generate more leads. On the other hand, if the foundation is weak, almost no traffic will be cost effective. For example, if you initially convert 1% of visitors, but through optimization can increase that conversion rate to 2%, you can literally cut the amount you spend on ads in half and still achieve the same result! Conversely, if your conversion rate drops from 2% to 1%, you'd have to spend twice the amount on ads to generate the same amount of sales.

Based on that, we are going to start by creating or enhancing that marketing foundation. This will ensure that any money spent on awareness building will have the best opportunity to convert the incoming prospects into paying customers.

The Website

The first part of this marketing foundation is a high-converting website. No surprise here as most of the marketing tactics we will be discussing will be interwoven into the website. For that reason, it's extremely important to make sure your site is up to snuff and that it either immediately converts the traffic and makes the sale or gets visitors plugged into a follow-up system. Unfortunately, many businesses simply use their websites to provide contact information and hope that any visitors that show up on the site will just call them which ends up leaving a lot of money on the table.

Credibility

The first goal is to create credibility for your message. The more you can do to create trust between you and your visitor, the better. As we discussed earlier, the more trust you build, the more receptive they are going to be to your marketing message.

So how do you create credibility in practice? To start with, the tone of your website (the look, feel, and content) should match the tone of your industry in general. It doesn't need to be super fancy, but it should at least give off a professional vibe. A law firm is not going to have a pink background with music just as a lawyer isn't going to show up in flip-flops and a t-shirt. It's all about presentation and making sure it gives off the right message.

Even though we shouldn't judge a book by its cover, we do, so it's best to get that straightened out by avoiding contradicting messages. That said, if your product or service is supposed to be fun, make the website a little bit fun. If you're selling fun and your website is bland, this will work against you. So again, it's all about the message you are trying to convey.

Video - The Easy Creibility Booster

Let's now move from the look of the website to the content of the website, starting with how it should be presented. These days, I highly recommend a combination of video and text. Videos are huge credibility builders, while text is great for quick reference material and helps you to get found by the search engines.

The reason that video is so powerful is because people can connect with people through video, not text on a page. This is especially important for companies in the B2B service spheres as you often "are" the product.

Instead of a boring About Us page that no one will ever read, put in a video that describes your company. Tell them why you do what you do. Tell them how you got started in the business. Don't make a sales pitch; just tell a story. Let the passion for your business come out.

The idea of getting on camera may make you nervous, but it shouldn't. The videos don't need to be incredible works of art; they just need to be professional. A smartphone has good enough video quality, so you just need a solid microphone.

Alright, so let's say you've now got a professional looking website template (or whatever feel you're going for) and I've convinced you on the benefits of using video on the website. You know how the material should be presented, but what pages/content should you be creating?

Content and Expectation Setting for Products and Services

A website typically has at least a Home page, About Us page, a Contact Us page, a Lead Capture page, a Products or Services page, and an optional Blog page. This is a good starting point that can be built upon later.

The homepage will simply serve as the main landing page for people who visit your website, usually by searching your company's name on Google or by typing your URL directly into the search bar. What you put on your Homepage is dependent on your industry and goals. Typically, it's good practice to welcome the visitor either through a video or text and give them a quick highlight of your offerings as well as the latest news from your company. Advanced users might integrate a lead capture strategy here, which we will get to later.

About Us Page: This was mentioned earlier, but to reiterate, the About Us page should tell your story in a compelling manner. Talk about how you got started and why you are in business. Try to include video and/or pictures of you and your staff and perhaps your facility.

Contact Us Page: This page is probably the easiest to create. Just provide your contact information and a little encouragement for readers to get in touch. If you want to go above and beyond that, you could consider putting in a web form and, perhaps, a map to your location. The web form, when submitted, will send the message directly to your email.

Product/Services Pages: Most product pages,

when selling a product or service, will simply list the features and then post the price. Some even just say call for quote. That is a huge mistake. People hate calling for quotes and, as a result, you can expect to lose a lot of visitors that way. Visitors will just assume it's too expensive and move on to a company that has more transparent pricing.

That said, in many industries, there is just no realistic way to provide a one size fits all quote. To get around this I've experimented with a few things and have had some good results. One thing is a quote calculator. The calculator would ask collect a variety of information that's needed for the quote, usually like quantities, features/services required, etc. It would then calculate a ballpark quote based on that data. One other thing to try is an RFQ page where the prospect could attach a print or requirements doc and then send it directly to sales for a fast response. Typically, these work significantly better than forcing them to call or go through a general contact us form even though there is little difference between them.

Beyond quoting calculators, for each of your products/services, consider posting a video of you describing the offering. Just like for the about page, showing is so much more powerful than telling. You can describe the benefits the customer will receive and tell them all about the amazing features. Also, don't forget to do a quick product demo to prove it can do what you say it can do. Tell them about your amazing guarantee or your unique selling proposition. This is your chance to set that expected value high so that they will select your product or service over your competitors. Moreover, don't lose sight of what you are really selling. If it's entertainment, share why it's going to be so entertaining. If it's relaxation, share why it will be so relaxing your customers.

Optional but highly recommended: Review Pages

If you've been in business for a while and have received some good feedback from past customers, consider either adding a review feature to your products page, or if you offer services, a testimonials page. These social proof pages fall into the "Other people" category of perception channels we talked about earlier and are extremely powerful. In later chapters, we will cover how to go about getting these reviews if you don't have them already.

Optional Blog Page

Many small businesses wonder if they should start a blog or not. Blogs are not mission critical but can provide significant value to those in certain service industries. Physical product sellers and commoditized services such as restaurants, however, will find they don't offer tremendous value.

Blogs are good conduits for news and for helping in your search engine rank, which we will discuss later. Since most physical product sellers and restaurants will have limited news of interest to announce to the world, it simply may not be worth putting the time into consistently blogging. And consistently blogging is unfortunately a prerequisite to getting any kind of benefit from a blog. On the more positive side though, blogs can also offer a content marketing opportunity where you could discuss industry news, delve more into depth of one of your offerings, or talk about upcoming releases of new products or features.

Landing/Squeeze Pages

A landing page allows you to capture information such as names and email addresses and will then automatically connect with your follow-up system. This goes far beyond what you'll typically see from a small business website, but is absolutely essential for a high converting website, or more broadly, a successful marketing campaign.

Typically, a landing page will look something like this: You go to a website and you're offered a free report on X in exchange for your email. You then opt in and they send you the report as promised. But in addition to the report, you're now receiving emails on a regular basis. Remember, this is extremely important since 80% of buyers aren't ready at this moment to buy, but certainly might be in the future. This allows you to continue to build influence and even more critically, maintain awareness.

Because of this fact, a landing page will be, perhaps, the most important part of your website, and so I highly recommend split testing your landing page many times to ensure you get the highest conversion rates possible.

Landing Page Design

Landing pages are designed with one goal: to capture the visitor's info. Typically, you will create an ad or other marketing material that will drive the prospect to your landing page and initiate the follow-up sequence. As you might imagine, most visitors don't give out their information willy-nilly, so you must entice them with some sort of bribe in order to get their information. We will cover creating your bribe in more detail in just a moment, but for now, let's assume you have some sort of bribe (like a free trial or sample of your product) ready to give out.

In terms of design, landing pages are designed to be very straightforward with no unnecessary clutter. If your goal is to capture prospects' email and give them something in return, the landing page should just consist of a headline, describing the offer, a box for them to type in their email, and a submit button. At most, you'll also have a very short paragraph talking about the offer, but that is it. No distractions. No clutter.

If you want to take your landing page to the next level, you can use a video sales letter, which, as you might imagine, is just a video that describes why the visitor should give you their email in exchange for the freebie. You'll typically achieve a higher conversion rate than if you did just a standard one with text, but they are more time-intensive.

Quick Tip: If you want to make your life much easier, I recommend you use a landing page creator that automatically integrates with your autoresponder/email software of choice such leadpages.

Bribe Creation

Let's circle back now and cover your bribe creation. What should you offer as a bribe? For starters, informational reports are easy to make and free to distribute. In real estate for example, Realtors can offer a free price analysis or a physical book or DVD on buying and selling real estate. I love this kind of education-based marketing because it builds credibility by setting you up as an informational authority.

Informational reports naturally work well for service-based businesses. But what if you sell physical products? Well, how about offering a sample? Can you offer a trial period? Or perhaps, you could offer some quality information on solving the underlying problem they are having, which causes them to look at your website in the first place.

My favorite example of this is a company called Discmakers. They sell custom DVDs and CDs. Naturally, you can't really give away samples of that nor can you offer a free trial. So what do they bait their visitors with? Well, they asked themselves who is most likely to buy our products and what are they using them for. The answer was small-time bands and indie filmmakers that sell those DVDs or CDs. So what they did was put out a great info course on how to drop and promote an album. Additionally, they also put together a great report on marketing for filmmakers to target that segment. All they ask in return is your email. The genius of this is twofold: first, they are providing something of real value to their readers, which alone is enough to get them to opt in. Second, the course itself helps the bands/filmmakers to sell more albums, and where do the albums come from? Discmakers, of course!

Hopefully, that gives you some ideas of what you can use as bait; if all else fails, you can always offer an instant quote or small discount and capture their email that way. In the end, the whole purpose is to put them on your email marketing list, which generates probably the highest ROI of any marketing tactic. The money is in the list they always say. I think they are right.

FOLLOW-UP SYSTEM

Once you have built your landing page, it's time to integrate your follow-up system and connect it to the completed landing page. As always, let's start with our focusing question: What exactly is the goal of a follow-up system? The follow-up system is designed to get potential customers to purchase your goods or service by staying top of mind through the continual building of perceived offering value. Doing this maximizes your efforts to bring people to your website and make a sale.

The type of follow-up system you implement will depend on your price point and how valuable each lead is. If you are selling a $10 product, you're not going to have an elaborate follow-up system in which you take your prospects out to eat and give them a call every week. You might, however, do something like that if they are considering signing a multi-year, multi-million dollar service agreement.

To start with, the absolute, most basic system is typically an automated email system that will send out a series of emails talking about the product or service that could culminate in a small discount if the person still hasn't purchased by the end of an initial email follow-up sequence. I recommend everyone start here and build out the system further if desired.

Automated Email Follow Up

The way the system typically works is that immediately after a prospect enters in their info into your landing page, an instant email should be sent out to them. Depending on what your bribe was, it could be the delivery of the free report as promised, or if it's a physical good, simply a confirmation that their information has been received and that you are processing their request.

After the initial email, the world is your oyster. You might find it helpful to map out the list of topics or subjects you want to cover before writing the actual emails. By doing it this way, you have a rough outline of what direction you want to take the email sequence in before getting bogged down in the writing and forgetting where you were going with it.

Here are a couple of ideas for the email sequence if you can't think of what you want to write about:

5 Tips to Fixing x - In this case, x is their problem and in each email, our bribe, since there is a good chance they will convert without having to discount. you cover one tip while simultaneously soft-selling your offering.

Product-related information - Basically, you'll provide testimonials, case studies, and additional information about your offering. This your more traditional "hard sell" route.

Weekly/Monthly Newsletter - To be quite honest, I usually wait until I run out of pre-planned content before I switch prospects over to a monthly newsletter. Local businesses have an advantage here, as they can talk about community events or local happenings. If you are, say, a SAAS company, most people won't care about what your company was doing last month, and even if they did, that information is probably better provided through a blog.

Discounts - If the prospect has been in your automatic email sequence for a month or two without buying, it might be worth offering a discount to push them over the edge. I don't recommend leading with a discount though, unless that was your bribe in the first place since there is a good chance they will convert without having to discount.

No matter what type of email follow-up sequence you end up using, it's important to use analytics to find out what kind of emails prospects are responding to. You can typically get this information from the email service provider you use. Speaking of...

Which Email Service Should you Use?

If you haven't done so already, it's now time

to load up your email follow-up sequence into your autoresponder/email service provider. People often debate which autoresponder is best, but in reality, it doesn't really matter too much as they all have similar functionality these days (just don't be sending it from your Gmail, Bccing everyone).

I usually just recommend choosing one of the bigger guys since they have more integration with other products like landing page creators. I personally like MailChimp because it's cheap and works with almost everything, but Aweber and Constant Contact are also good albeit more expensive options

No matter what provider you go with, the key to a good email marketing system is consistency. Write the emails in advance and schedule them out about a couple of days to a week apart. Too many mailings will cause people to opt out, but too few will get lost in the crowded inbox.

Expanding your Follow-Up System (Optional)

Now that you have the most cost-effective follow-up system on the planet, it's time to build out the rest of the system if you desire to do so. For some, this is where the wooing ends. For others, it's just getting started. Here are some additional ideas you can consider using in your follow-up system. Again, this will be highly dependent on your price point. I would not recommend doing any of these unless your price point or LCV is $500+.

Direct Mail - I'm a huge advocate of this one.

By sending literally anything in the mail, you'll be able to stand out from most of your competition. The reason is, 80% of your offline competition doesn't do it and 99% of your online competition doesn't do it.

What you send could be as simple as a handwritten thank you card saying thank you for the inquiry, a typed quote on high-quality paper along with your business card, or it could even be a complete sequence of follow-up letters. The great thing is, it not only stands out but you can be quite sure it gets read or at least skimmed. Some might be turned off to direct mail given the expense, but ROI can easily be measured to determine if it is suitable.

Freebies – Typically, physical in nature, these don't necessarily have to be related to your industry. You could send someone a $5 Starbucks gift card or a nice pen. Research has repeatedly shown that if you do something nice for someone, the recipient typically feels like they should reciprocate. With any luck, that reciprocation will include buying your product or service! Some might call it bribery; I call it making people feel special.

Physical Interaction - If you are selling a high-end product or service, you can consider following up by phone call or even taking the person out to dinner as mentioned earlier. As human interaction is hard to scale, it should be reserved for select customers or for those in the very high price points.

Follow-Up Sequencing

The key to the follow-up process, beyond consistency, is to take a mixed approach. Don't just call every day for a week and let that be it. People don't appreciate being harassed, and nothing comes off more like harassment than the repeated use of the same medium, particularly calling. Instead, you could start the email sequence by telling your prospects that you are sending them a special gift in the mail. In the mail a few days later could be that small gift along with a strong pitch for your services followed by a short handwritten note saying thank you for checking us out. A week later, you could follow up with a phone call. Heck, you could do it all in the same week and it would still come off much better than three calls in three days.

How often to reach out and by what medium should be studied by you to determine what works best in your industry. But I like Keller Williams' approach as a starting point, which is eight times in eight weeks using mixed mediums. If after that they still haven't taken any action, then just follow up once a month for twelve months. Whatever you do, make sure you first create a calendar of how each engagement should play out. If using the 8x8 plan, you would map out how you would engage with the prospect on a weekly basis and then on the monthly plan.

An example of this would be: Week one- Phone call. Ask if they got my letter. Week two- Email. Thank them for talking with you. Week three:

In-person meeting - Discuss proposal, etc.

After you plan out your schedule, you need to be able to track who is where in the follow-up sequence to stay organized. You could do this in your head, though I really don't recommend this as it becomes really hard to remember and keep track of everyone. For those with a small-to-medium number of prospects, a simple excel sheet or folder will do. Alternatively, if you have a good number, it might be wise to track them using a CRM solution.

POST-SALE RETENTION AND ENGAGEMENT

Once you have completed a sale and delivered the product, you've done the hard part of building awareness, convincing them to buy by selling the value, and then meeting those expectations (hopefully). At this point, you could simply move on to try and do something similar with the next potential customer, or you could keep in touch with the customer in hopes that he or she will buy from you in the future.

For nearly all businesses, it will be significantly cheaper and more effective to market to customers that have already bought from you. The reason for this is simple; they've already been sold on your product and they have personal experience telling them what they can expect from it. Assuming that experience went good, you won't have to sell them on your value again. You simply must remind them you exist. You can take advantage of the situation by implementing a customer retention pipeline to standardize the post-sale marketing and engagement to achieve some pretty great outcomes.

Customer Retention Pipeline

Originally, I hadn't planned to discuss retention in much depth, but after some discussions with startup founders, I realized the importance of including a more in-depth discussion. Many businesses have a burn-and-churn mentality. That is, once the sale has been consummated, the business would cease all wooing and move onto acquiring new customers. Established businesses are less likely than startups to fall into this trap because they typically have more than one offering, so they know they can get additional revenue out of the customer, but even they are missing the point.

If you recall, there are three drivers of perception about your product: What the company says, the customer's personal experience, and what other people say about the product or service. That last one is key for us here. By leveraging our existing customers, we can use them to spread the word about our offering.

The key is to then keep your customers engaged and happy so that when the time comes, they'll love the opportunity to share the word about your products or services. That doesn't even take into account, of course, the fact that they very well might buy from you again if they stay engaged.

At all stages of the customer pipeline, we want to be continually building awareness at the very least. While it doesn't take nearly as much marketing spend to maintain awareness (or create engagement), it is still important to remind the customer that you exist from time to time. In many service-based businesses, this is just sending out something like a Christmas card, an annual checkup reminder, a thank-you card, etc. However, many businesses will want to take a more proactive approach to keep users engaged and aware. The question is, since they already know about your business and offering, what should your approach be?

Discounts and Gamification

One of the most commonly used approaches is to offer discounts on your other products/services to the customer. This could be a cross-sell or upsell. Naturally, this approach requires you to have an existing product line or a consumable and wouldn't really work for SaaS companies that only have one service.

The interesting thing about these discounts, though, is that almost no customer loyalty programs when pulled off wisely are just a straightforward discount on goods or services. Typically, if it's just "10% off" type of message, it comes off as an ad. However, if it is a buy 10 and get one free type of deal, it's perceived as a lot more exciting for some reason, even though it's objectively the same, if not a worse offer.

The benefit of a customer loyalty program is two-fold. First, they provide both an incentive to come back but also provide a way to keep customers engaged. They do this through clever schemes designed to reward customer loyalty by providing something free after a certain amount of purchases. It can be as simple as punch cards that can get redeemed for a free ice cream after five visits or as elaborate as Starbucks' star game that gives a free drink after collecting enough stars. However, as you can see, the end result is just a discount no matter how it's implemented. Because of that, no matter what you do, be sure to have fun with it and make it fun for your customers as well. Below are some ideas to get you started:

The Classic: This rewards the customer with something after a set number of visits. Since it rewards based on the number of visits, typically, it's used in physical stores.

Mystery Cards - I thought this one was pretty creative. Once I was at a restaurant during the Christmas season, and after the meal, I was given a red envelope and told to come back in January and bring the envelope. If we brought it back unopened, we would get a certain discount/gift card ranging from $5 all the way to $500, depending on what was in the envelope.

Big Spender - In this setup, you reward the customer with points based on how much they spend. Once they have a certain amount of points, they can redeem them for something. To make it more exciting, modify the way points are earned. If Tuesdays are typically slow, give out twice as many points for dollar spent on Tuesdays.

VIP Treatment/Loyalty Tiers - Made famous by airlines and hotels, this type of program makes the guest feel special by giving them complimentary upgrades to those in certain tiers of their loyalty program. Since it is usually done on an availability basis, there is really no additional cost in offering this. If a hotel has a dozen suites available that they know will not be booked that night, why not give a free upgrade to some of their best guests? Alternatively, something like a spa could offer an additional service like a pedicure for free to their best customers.

Challenger: This one made famous by Starbucks gamifies the loyalty program by setting challenges for the customers to complete. Typically, these involve coming for a certain number of days in a row or for buying a certain item. Completing these challenges will reward stars that can be used for those free drinks.

Sampler - If you have a large product line that lends itself well to samples, consider sending out samples of your other products when you mail out the order. Everyone loves free stuff, and they might just like it so much they order a full-size version of the sample.
The Giver - Here's an interesting one. After the sale, send the customer a gift card they can give to one of

their friends. You will not only endear the customer but also potentially pick up a new one as well. To even further incentivize, you can even offer something to the first customer if the potential customer uses the gift card.

Good Customer Service – Perhaps, the cheapest yet most effective retention plan is to simply offer good customer service. Customers will almost always forgive a company for making a mistake if they are apologetic and work quickly to make it right. If the customer service experience is poor, expect to lose a customer for life and for the person to tell all their friends about the negative experience too.

On the other hand, if you really want to blow your customers away, use incredible customer service even when there is no problem at all. What do I mean by that? I mean reaching out personally and checking with them on how their experiences with the product is going and if there is anything you can do to make it better. For example, you could send a simple handwritten note to individual customers. Not only does this put a smile on their faces but it opens the door for very helpful feedback. This is especially helpful for startups who are just finding their way and really need that early feedback. While obviously this isn't sustainable for businesses with thousands of customers, consider doing it for a select few. For more on this concept, read Paul Graham's "Do Things that Don't Scale".

AWARENESS BUILDING

At this point, the website should be up and the funnel optimized from initial lead capture through follow up through retention. You are ready to turn on the traffic nozzle and start capturing customers (not literally, of course). This is where the real fun begins, and likely the reason you bought this book.

In the next section, we will be discussing a variety of tactics to build awareness for your offering and how you can drive people to your website or business. We'll start with online methods such as social media and then move to some offline methods with an integrated online twist. With that, let's jump right in!

Social Media

As social media tends to dominate the marketing conversation these days, it seemed only right to start with it. Social media has as many skeptics as it has fans. Some swear by it; some don't buy the hype. As with most things, the truth lies somewhere in the middle. While a correct use of social media can be used fairly effectively to work toward your marketing goals, it should definitely not be seen as the only route to success or even required for success. In fact, I've only ever met one business owner who uses social media as the end-all-be-all of their marketing. All that to say, if you absolutely hate the idea of using social media, not only do you not have to use it, you probably **shouldn't** use it. That goes for all the awareness building channels, not just social media.

With that said, let's dive into social media and break it down. The term social media marketing is very broad, but we can break it down into roughly two marketing groups: free and paid. Free social media, such as a Facebook page, Twitter page, or Instagram page are all good engagement tools. That is, they are better suited for keeping awareness rather than building it directly. There are exceptions to this, of course, which we will discuss. But in most cases, think of it more as part of your follow-up/customer-loyalty pipeline, where you can market to those who have already taken interest in your company.

The other type, paid social media marketing, like Facebook ads, is where the real power of social media is on the awareness building front. Let's now break social media marketing down, platform by platform, and put together an action plan that can be incorporated to drive the views to your website as well as maintain that awareness through engagement.

Establishing Your Social Media Presence

The first step you'll want to take is to decide what platforms you want to spend your time developing. I think the most common mistake businesses make is that they try to do too much, too early. They establish about 5 brand pages all in one day and are instantly overwhelmed by trying to manage them. For that reason, I highly recommend you just pick one or two to start with based on your business. You can always establish more later.

Platform Overviews:

Facebook: Facebook is the grandad of all social media and is well suited for most brands. Having a business page and posting high-quality content can be a good strategy if you have proper expectations. As mentioned earlier, Facebook, like the other platforms in their free forms, should be primarily viewed as an engagement platform (similar to email) and not directly an awareness building one. This is especially true as of late because, a few months ago, Facebook changed their news feed algorithm to suppress the posts from businesses in order to, allegedly, make content from family and friends more visible. My take on it is that it's a simple pay to play cash grab, but regardless, it is the new reality.

There is, however, an exception to the idea that Facebook simply engages. When people share or like something, your content has the opportunity to be seen by people who haven't already "liked" your brand. This is free advertising for you when it happens. But the unfortunate reality for most businesses is that their content will never go viral, and as a result, they are unlikely to reach people beyond the immediate scope of their fan base. The best you can do is create engaging and "shareable" content and hope it gets, well, shared.

The chicken, the egg, and shareable content

I've been running a test for about a year or so on one of my business page to see how many likes I can get without using any paid traffic sources. Instead of paying, every day, high-quality content is posted to the page. Since I started the experiment, the page has achieved a laughable 34 likes. This brings us to the chicken or the egg problem. You can't get new fans or likes without having existing fans liking the content you are posting.

The best solution that I've found for this is to spend the money up front to grow the number of people liking your page to a respectable number. After that, focus on putting out that high-quality content, engaging your fans, and hope that the content is shared. This strategy will allow you to minimize the cash outlay required to sustain your growth.

Twitter:

Twitter is like having a giant megaphone and yelling at anyone who will listen. Many brands use it effectively to share the latest news of their business, to get feedback from clients, or start trouble (just follow Wendy's for a hilarious example).

Most of the rules for posting to Facebook apply to Twitter. Keep it short, and keep it interesting. The only difference is post frequency. Typically, people tweet (post to Twitter) much more often than they will post to Facebook. For that reason, you'll need to tweet more often to stay relevant as you'll quickly get drowned out by the other megaphone wielders if you don't.

Other than that, follow those who follow your business and reach out to have a chat with them once in a while to solicit their feedback. If there is one thing Twitter is useful for, it's for being a constant source of very honest feedback. The feedback they can give is not only helpful (sometimes) but you can count on the fact they'll be telling their friends they had a chat with your brand, especially if it's of decent size.

This might sound funny coming from a guy who does marketing for a living, but I'm not personally a huge fan of Twitter. I find the required tweet frequency exhausting and often the user base is a bit more, er "honest" (read hostile) than Facebook's community. But like I said at the beginning, it's important to find the platforms you want to use and those you don't. I know people who love to tweet and see great results from it. It's just not my cup of tea.

Instagram:

Instagram has been soaring in popularity as of late. From fitness models to Fortune 500 companies, everyone seems to want a piece of the action. Instagram can be used very effectively for brands that are visual. Painters, Realtors, landscapers, and many other types of local businesses can see strong results from Instagram. If, however, you are a software startup or B2B company, you're not likely to gain much from posting to Instagram unless it's about your sweet ping-pong tables.

LinkedIn:
LinkedIn is the B2B dream. It allows you to connect to exactly the right people you need in order to promote your business. There are three basic ways you can use LinkedIn effectively.

The first is using it as an authority building platform using the posts feature. Articles published on LinkedIn tend to get a higher number of views from business people and decision-makers. Typically, the posts are longer in nature and contain some solid insights, which is why they are more widely read from these type of people vs say a Facebook post.

The second way to utilize LinkedIn is as a connection tool. Basically, it entails simply "connecting" with a number of prospects and then messaging them. The strategy has mixed results though, as entrepreneurs, in particular, are particularly inundated with marketing people trying to sell them stuff. That said, you can achieve some pretty good results if you choose your connections strategically and offer value upfront.

YouTube:
YouTube is another platform that I think most, if not all, businesses can benefit from. The added bonus of YouTube is that it's not just an engagement platform even in its free form like the others. Videos have a much better chance of being seen by people who have never seen your brand before, and they don't have to even go viral for them to do so since YouTube benefits from a lot of organic (free) traffic based on the keywords in your video. We will cover video marketing in more depth later and why it's so good at building awareness. But for now, just know that this is one platform you should really consider utilizing.

Paid Social Media Traffic

In order to get your brand in front of people who don't already know about it, paid methods are the way to go. Like before, there are a variety of options to choose from. The nice thing about paid ads, however, is that you can run test campaigns on different platforms and compare results. You don't need to commit to a year of intensive social media posting in order to effectively compare them.

Facebook
When people first dabble into paid social media ads, it's usually through boosting a Facebook post. This is often for a good reason - Facebook has a

very refined audience targeting tool that will allow you to laser-focus on your targeted demographic.

The key requirement for Facebook ads is that you must know your target audience very well. Unlike Google AdWords, which we will cover later, you can't just target people searching for your type of business, like "Chinese Food in Walnut Creek". Instead, you must know the type of people that are interested in your Chinese restaurant in Walnut Creek.

Facebook Ad Creation

For best results, you shouldn't actually boost posts directly, but instead, always use the ad creation tool. Otherwise, you miss out on important tools and limit your results. Once you open the ad creation tool, create your ad based on your goal, whether that is app installs, video views, post engagement, conversions, etc.

From my personal testing, I have found the best two goals to be conversion and post engagement. Conversion typically means you get the sale or get the squeeze page opt-in. Post engagement, on the other hand, works very well for event ads. Surprisingly, traffic seems to be the weakest option and is typically just like a weak form of conversions.

Unfortunately, to use Facebook's best option, conversions, you need to install what is called a Facebook "Pixel" into your website. Facebook has a guide on doing this, but it is a bit complicated. Fortunately, if you use something like WordPress, it isn't too difficult to install. Simply use the

"Add new" plugin option to search for a Facebook pixel plugin. Then copy and paste the pixel code from Facebook. After selecting your goal, you then focus on targeting the right potential customers as mentioned earlier. You can sort by location, demographics, interests, and more. You can even target people who like your competitors! You can see why, though, you absolutely must have an idea of who will be receptive to your offer or else you risk wasting a lot of money on people who will never buy.

Quick Tip: If you have different types of people that are interested in your products or services, then you can create an ad to target those different types of people.

Ad Design

Next, you must choose your ad design. I've had success with both single image and video ads. It's really up to you what format you want to use. Since image ads are typically easier to start with, most will begin there and experiment with video ads as time goes on.

Finally, you must decide what your messaging or offer is going to be. If you created that bribe we were talking about earlier, this is a great time to advertise that and bring people to your landing page. People love free stuff and it's a great way to break the ice with a new customer. It's usually easier to get them to take a small action like giving you their email instead of going directly for the sale. This is especially true if you have a high price point product. Once the email is captured, they would then be put into your follow-up system, which will greatly increase the odds of the sale being made.

Budget

One final consideration is the budget. Like before, there's nothing set in stone. Usually, I like to take it slow and set it at $1-$5 per day initially. If the ad proves itself, you can always increase it. This strategy will allow you to create and test multiple ads on the cheap. As for bidding on the CPM (Cost per 1k impressions) or CPC (Cost per click), just let Facebook automatically optimize for it. They usually do a good job putting their disturbing amount of data to use for their advertisers benefit.

Measuring ad Performance

It's important to have an objective measurement for evaluating your ads. Facebook allows you to look at ad performance and see what kind of conversions you are getting from each ad. It goes without saying that if you are losing money on ads, you should probably stop running them or change your ad.

Even good ads will start to become stale after a while. This drop off can take two weeks or two months, but it will happen. For this reason, you should evaluate your ads performance at least weekly to ensure you are still getting an acceptable return. Finally, you'll want to split-test different headlines, images, and content in order to create a truly effective ad. Hopefully, you'll do this early on before you put too much money into ads!

Facebook Retargeting Ads

Before we move on to other social media platforms, I want to highlight one type of ad that is different from the other Facebook ads - Retargeting ads. I love these ads because they work and work well. If you've ever been to a website such as Amazon and looked at a toaster, only to find that toaster to follow you over to Facebook, you've experienced retargeting. It's a powerful tool and can greatly increase your conversion rate. The downside is that it can be somewhat tricky to implement.

To start, set up a Facebook pixel on your website like you do for the conversions goal, but instead of using the normal targeting, use the custom audience option. You can then have a variety of options to choose from in terms of how they interacted with your brand. For example, if they put something in their shopping cart but did not check out, you could run a retargeting ad that would target those people by asking them if they would like to complete their checkout. If they click on the ad, you could then take them back to their cart for checkout.

Retargeting in Real Estate Usage Example

Here's another quick example: I've done some retargeting for homeowners who visit a Realtor's website and so are theoretically interested in selling their home. We then follow them over to Facebook and constantly remind them that if they ever decide to sell, they should definitely sell with this Realtor. Our ultimate goal, of course, is for them to click the retargeting ad and fill out either a contact form on the website or request a home valuation because once we know who they are, we can put them in the follow-up pipeline.

Twitter Ads

If Twitter is more your style, it also has many ad options to choose from. You can choose from sponsoring a tweet, promoting your business to get more followers, or even promoting a trend. Given that the later costs about $200k the last time I checked, most businesses will opt for either promoted tweets or promoted accounts.

Even given those two, I think promoted tweets will provide the most value as they can drive people to landing pages in a similar manner to a Facebook ad. Given this is Twitter, though, you need to be cognizant of the character limit, unlike on Facebook. One advantage Twitter has over Facebook is slightly lower CPM. Facebook simply has more advertisers competing for a limited number of ad slots and, as a result, the prices there are usually higher.

Influencers

Ironically, perhaps the best use of Twitter ads isn't through Twitter itself, but from big names on Twitter who you can work with to promote your brand. For prices from $5 to $50,000 you can get an "influencer" to tweet your ad to their followers.

Usually it will come in the form of a recommendation to their followers regarding your product or service.

The key here is to know your target demographic and the demographic of the influencer you are considering. If your audiences are aligned, then you might have a good fit and wish to approach the influencer. While influencer marketeering is still in its infant stage, it's hard to dispute their results when the campaigns are executed well. For a prime example of this, look no further than the Fyre festival which was promoted almost entirely by popular influencers albeit mostly Instagram influencers. We'll discuss influencers later in the affiliate section, but for now, let's proceed on to Instagram.

Instagram Ads

One lovely thing about Instagram, from a marketing perspective, is that they were purchased by Facebook, so ad creation and management is a breeze. You create the ad the same as you do for Facebook, but simply check the Instagram box under placement. No need to learn more than one ad platform!

The other great thing about Instagram ads is that despite the fact that it's connected to Facebook, fewer advertisers choose to push ads to Instagram for whatever reason. As a result, it usually has a lower CPM cost. Additionally, from my time running ads, I've noticed my ads for Instagram tend to get more engagement vs the same ad on Facebook, but just slightly lower conversion rates.

The biggest thing to keep in mind about Instagram is the larger focus on the visual aspects of the ad (say more with the image, use less words). This is natural since Instagram is a visual-based platform. As a result, adopt an ad style that matches their Instagrammers' ad taste.

Just as in the case of Twitter, Instagram has a huge influencer scene that can be tapped for difference campaigns. Given the visual nature of Instagram though, the influencers here are more concentrated in Lifestyle, Fitness, and Vacationing. I apologize I cannot make that last category more concrete, but there are people who just go on a bunch of vacations and post pictures from exotic locations.

LinkedIn Ads

Need to build more awareness for your B2B company? Look no further than LinkedIn ads. With these, you can start generating leads in no time. To start with, you've got your typical display ads that allow you to target your ideal customer as well as sponsored InMail, which allows you to send messages directly to those customers you want to target like discussed before.

Beyond display ads, LinkedIn recently released LinkedIn premium. Thanks to LinkedIn premiums InMail feature, instead of waiting for prospects to accept your connection request first, you can send a direct message to them.

Here's the tactic breakdown: Find your prospects, then find something in common with them that you can use to break the ice. As before, you should then tell them how what you do benefits them and perhaps, invite them to coffee or, at the very least, start a dialogue. Don't forget that fundamentally, marketing is truly a numbers game, and if you do that a couple of times a week, you'll likely have tremendous success.

Social Media Ads Recap

I realize we covered a lot very quickly in terms of ad platforms. However, I don't want to waste your time with a step-by-step guide to setting up an ad for each platform, which has been covered ad nauseam by others. Instead, I want to focus on covering some of the primary options available to you, and as you can already see, there are many options available. The key then is to figure out which ad platform(s) fit in your awareness and influence-building strategy. That is to say, you need to experiment with platforms to see where you get the highest ROI and then double down on that platform. Getting a 200% ROI for ads on Facebook, but only 20% on Twitter? Well, then dump twitter and run more ads on Facebook!

Google Paid Advertising

Before moving on from online ads, I cannot avoid mentioning Google. Its advertising platform comes in a variety of flavors. Which one you pursue will really depend on your type of business. Google ads don't tend to focus on what the demographics of a potential client are as much as what they want right now.

Search Ads - For example, the core of Google's ad platform is search advertising with Google AdWords. Essentially, when a person searches something like "Mattresses", a mattress seller can pay to put their business on the top of the page. The key difference between this platform and, say, Facebook, is that Facebook targets the people who might be searching for mattresses given certain distinctions like demographics and search history, whereas Google ads primarily target people who are searching for mattresses this very moment. As a result, Google search ads are typically much more expensive.

Video Ads - Video ads are usually served before or during YouTube videos. Unlike search ads, people usually aren't looking to buy the moment the ad is served, but rather it's more interest-based. That said, you can get pretty creative when using video ads. For example, since you can actually select which videos you want your ad to run on, you can potentially run the ad while someone is doing research on products that you are selling. For example, if you are a computer company, you could run an ad on a video about the top five desktop computers of 2018. Alternatively, you could simply target videos in which the target demographics match your target demographics.

Adwords Express- I have not seen too many of these ads, but they push your local business to the top of the local search results as well as keywords that they select for you. I do not recommend using these as the costs are currently exorbitant and the results are unimpressive considering the alternatives such as search ads.

Display Ads: Similar to the video ads, these ads can be used to target the type of content being consumed or particular demographics. Generally regarded as inferior to search ads, the costs are a bit cheaper, but not enough for me to recommend them considering the prevalence of click fraud (Website owners who, one way or another, get people to click on the ads on their website without genuine interest in what is being advertised).

Other Major Online Ad plforms to consider:

Spotify/Pandora: Lastly, it's worth mentioning that the two music juggernauts are slowly rolling out a self-service ad platform. Similar to radio ads, these ads have the added benefit of better tracking and targeting metrics. They also make creating ads incredibly easy. You can either create one yourself or have your ad professionally narrated. While both are invite-only at the moment, keep it in the back of your mind since this will soon become a solid advertising option.

Search Engine Optimization

If someone searches Google for "Towels" and you happen to sell towels, wouldn't it be great if people would be directed to your website? Wouldn't it even be better if you didn't have to pay $1.50 for every person who clicks on your website like you do with Google Adwords? Well if you rank high enough in the search results, you can do exactly that. Breaking into the top 10 search results for competitive keywords, is unfortunately notoriously difficult. While there are no shortcuts to success, you can better your results through search engine optimization.

Search Engine Optimization is the art of optimizing your website to show up higher in the search results. Even though there are many search engines, most people just use this as a general way to refer to showing up in Google search results.

Naturally, ranking on Google is the dream of any marketer. Unfortunately for most, that's all it ever is. I often laugh when I see companies looking for a "SEO master". The only people with any true SEO knowledge are Google employees that designed the ranking algorithm. The rest of us simply try and follow the "Best SEO practices" and pray to get lucky. Those best practices fall into two categories: On page and off-page optimization.

On-Page SEO

On-page factors include the title of the page, keywords used, keyword density, and website content. In our towel example, if you were trying to rank in the search engine for the term "Towels", you should correspondingly have a page called Towels. On your towel page, you should also use the word towels a fair bit so there is no confusion that your page is, in fact, about towels. Moreover, on your Towel page, you should probably have a picture of a towel and even include a video.

You'll also often see people buy a domain with the keyword they are trying to rank for. This is a smart move, as it will increase the ranking of the website and some people just type in the generic term and add .com to the end. This is also why some domain names go for hundreds of thousands of dollars. And in case you are wondering, towels.com is taken by Bounty. Sorry.

Finally, Google takes into account the total website content. Generally, the more content you have, the better. It's even better if that content also has something to do with the keyword you are trying to rank. For example, you could have a "Top 5 towels" page or "Top factors to consider when towel shopping".

There are some other factors that seem to make a difference such as internal linking structure, but I don't think it's worth your time trying to find every nuanced on-page SEO tactic. You are better served creating high quality content themed around your niche that caters to real visitors.

Off-Page SEO

Even if you hit on-page optimization perfectly, you won't likely get very far without off-page optimization. Off-page SEO basically comes down to three things: the number of people linking to you, the words they use as anchor text when they link to you, and the authority of those domains linking to you.

Unfortunately, you can't really control any of that, which is why SEO is so hard to begin with. There are only three strategies that I am aware of that work with any kind of reliability. The first is guest blogging. In this instance, you approach or email someone that owns a blog in the same niche as you. Ask them if they accept guest posts, and if they do, you would write up a post and then include a link back to your personal website. Just be sure that when you are linking back to your own website that you use the keyword you are trying to rank for as the anchor text. For example, if you are a real estate agent, don't link it as joerealtor.com but as Florida Realtor so that when clicked, it takes them to your website. Not only do you get the link for this but you also might get readers from the other website that are interested in learning more about you or your company. The second method is what we call shareable content. Content so good (or controversial) that people will link to you without you asking them for it. They might say, "Hey did you see the article over on joerealtor.com's website about the housing crisis?" and then include a link to Joe's website. By doing so, they link to you and give you more authority in Google's eyes. Given all the clickbait as of late though, this method may be beginning to lose steam.

The final method is creating videos and including your link in the description. I've had a fair bit of success with this one. If your video gets embedded or shared on other websites, often times, your link will come with it, bringing more authority to your website along with visitors that watched the video.

Word of Warning: Don't try to rank for anything generic like "weight loss" or "towels". You will quite literally be going up against the top marketers around as well as some of the largest companies in the world. These fights simply are not winnable. Instead, go after longer phrases for the keyword you are trying to rank for. Instead of "Supplements" try "Best organic protein shakes". There is a lot less search engine volume, but at least, you have a chance to rank for it unlike the former.

Local Ranking

Let's now move away from traditional search engine marketing and look at a very powerful subset - Local Ranking. Have you ever googled something like "Pizza Restaurants in New York" with the goal of finding a solid pizza place near you? If so, you have seen a list of three restaurants with their map locations and performed what is called a local search. Obviously, any New York Pizzeria wants to be in that top spot for the pizza in New York search because of the massive amounts of free exposure. Fortunately, it's not just pizza shops that can benefit from local search, but any local business with a physical presence. Local searches differ from traditional search engine marketing because they factor in the location of the individual searching and the location of the businesses matching the search.

For example, the global search term "Mattresses" is a lot different than "Mattress sellers in New York". The first is a global search term, where there would be much more competition compared to later where the competition is only between mattress sellers in New York. Moreover, we also know that there are some key differences between Google's regular search algorithm and their local search algorithm. Because of those reasons, ranking locally is typically easier to do. **Hint**: If what you're searching for returns results with a map, it's a local search.

As mobile search volume continues to increase, local search rankings become much more important. Fortunately, very few businesses are taking advantage of local search, which is great for any business looking to jump in since the competition is much less fierce.

Now that you understand the difference between local and global searches, let's talk about how to start getting your ranking in local search up. The first thing you'll want to do is verify your Google listing. You can do this by going to Business.Google.com. From there, simply type in your business name/address and you should be able to find it. If not, you can add it manually. Usually, they will send you a postcard or verify via telephone to claim the listing. This will link your Google profile to your business listing. Once you've claimed it, you can start filling out the listing. Next, you should upload pictures, fill in store hours, and use the new post feature. All of these things typically help the ranking.

After that, it's time to start building citations and links. Citations are any mention of your business on the web such as your company name, address, and phone number. Links are simply links to your website as we discussed earlier. Link and citation building are pretty time-intensive and not something you want to spend your personal time on. Instead, consider looking for people offering these services on Fiverr or SEO Clerks for help with this. A general principle when it comes to link building is quality over quantity. 1000 bad links are probably going to be worse for your ranking than 10 good links.

The next thing you'll want to do is to put together a strategy for gathering reviews. Reviews on Google, Yelp, and even Facebook are now pretty important. After a successful transaction, you could email your client a list of places they could post a review and tell them that you would really appreciate it if they left you a review. You'd be surprised how many people will post a review if you ask nicely. If all else fails, you can always bribe them in exchange for an honest review (usually by offering a freebie or discount on their next purchase). The more reviews that are coming in on a consistent basis, the better your results are going to be.

Beyond this, on-page optimization seems to have similar importance in local search. As long as you have semi-decent on-page SEO, you should be fine. Similarly, social signals in the form of customer engagement from Facebook, YouTube, etc. also seem to help, but you should have that covered already too if you have decided to start using social media to promote your business.

Amazon Search Engine Optimization

While we are on the topic of search engines, Amazon is, in fact, a massive product search engine and worth discussing. Used properly, Amazon can bring massive exposure and sales. However, if you offer a service or are a local business, feel free to skip this section.

For those interested in selling on Amazon, it is a pretty straightforward process. You list your product on Amazon by uploading a picture, setting a price, filling out a short description and then once a customer places an order, either you or Amazon ships the product.

Many product sellers opt to sell through Amazon because of their fulfillment network and wide exposure, myself included. Unfortunately, many sellers list their products on Amazon only to achieve disappointing results. The reason is, if you are not listed highly on Amazon for a particular product search, you won't get many sales. But if you don't get many sales, you won't rank high. You can probably see the problem.

The good news is, there is a solution to this chicken and the egg problem.

To start with, if you actually want to have hope with ranking, make sure you have Amazon ship your products using fulfillment by Amazon. Fulfillment by Amazon works by shipping your products to Amazon's warehouse in bulk and then they mail it out individually when orders come through. The benefits of this cannot be overstated. First, you rank higher than people that don't. Second, you don't have the headache of shipping it out every single time an order is placed. No need to worry who will ship when you are on vacation. Third, many people, like myself, will only buy something that is eligible for prime. Therefore, many people will just overlook your product once they see that it is not eligible for prime. The only downside is that it does cost a little bit more, but it is well worth it as you'll make more sales anyway.

While Amazon's ranking system is also a black box, it's a little more straightforward than Google. Naturally, products with more sales rank higher than those that don't. So how do you get more sales? Well, to start with, you need reviews.

People don't buy products without seeing some reviews first. Depending on the product you are selling, Amazon has some programs that help you get those first couple of reviews in exchange for a free or discounted product. Otherwise, you could reach out to past customers and see if they are willing to post a review for you. Reviews are powerful because they not only help increase sales but also, from my experience, help with the rankings themselves. If you are really having trouble getting reviews, consider sending some Facebook traffic to your website and asking readers if they will give you a review in exchange for a discount.

After getting 5-10 initial reviews, it's time to start pushing some traffic to your product. You can do this through Amazon's sponsored products or through other paid traffic method such as Facebook ad or Google ad. The cost of paid advertising will be high initially, but as sales start to come through on your Amazon product page, your ranking will get higher and as a result, more sales will start to come through organically, which will increase your margins dramatically. When I was selling my product on Amazon, I went from nothing to $800 a day in just a couple of months, though I did have a pretty unique product which did help.

Quick Tip: It's always smart to check Amazon's policies on review generation before starting a campaign. They are known to change them suddenly and then ban sellers who break the new rules.

ADVANCED MARKETING IDEAS

With the foundational stuff out of the way, we can now start talking about some non-traditional stuff. Well, perhaps, some of it is traditional, but we are going to be putting a new twist on it. Thanks to the website and built-in follow-up system, we can now integrate some pretty killer offline marketing tactics. As the whole world grows more obsessed with digital, you can really stand out by using a multi-channel approach.

Direct Mail Marketing

You really don't get more old-fashioned than traditional postcard marketing. Most marketers these days have completely disregarded it entirely. That's good for us because as email inboxes become more and more cluttered, mailboxes have become less and less cluttered. Nearly every postcard gets read, whereas you'd be lucky to get a 25% open rate with email.

Direct mail has traditionally had three major problems that limited its effectiveness: lack of targeting options, high cost, and inability to measure results in any meaningful way. Thanks to a variety of advances in the industry and our foundational digital setup, we can overcome these obstacles and make the humble postcard one of the deadliest marketing tools in our arsenal.

The first problem most people have is the targeting issue. While shotgun marketing can work for local businesses, product or targeted service-based companies will likely struggle with that approach since they have a more narrowly defined target market. However, thanks to everyone's favorite boogeyman, big data, we can buy lists that target our ideal customer. For starters, Experian sells some fantastic lists. You can sort by target income, geography, interests, type of living situation, and more. The best part is, the lists are pretty cheap, usually just 10 cents per prospect.

For now, let's discuss another common complaint - the high cost of direct mail marketing. A printed and mailed postcard will typically run you 50 to 70 cents per mailing. One great strategy to lower costs is to buy the postcards in bulk, say 12 months' worth. By doing so, you'll save roughly 50% on the per piece price ($.03 vs 0.06 on Uprint). The reason is, printers give massive discounts for higher purchase quantity because of the high setup costs they incur and relatively low marginal unit costs. As a result, you'll save a lot by buying upfront.

Once you have your list and have purchased your postcards, you are ready to go. This approach will work great for those who have very specific customers in mind that are usually spread-out geographically. On the other hand, your customers are located geographically clustered, then you should definitely consider Every Door Direct Mail as an alternative in order to reduce costs further.

Every Door Direct Mail

Generally, the most expensive part of direct mailing is the mailing cost, not the printing. By using EDDM you can blanket a neighborhood for only 18 cents (postcard printing not included) as opposed to between $0.35 and $0.55. The big kicker is it's not only cheaper, but you can send massive 8 ½ by 11 "postcards" as opposed to the tiny 4x6 traditional postcards that you're probably used to seeing.

If you use a good printing company, like Uprinting, you can get a massive 8 ½ by 11 postcard for only 13-25 cents depending on the order quantity. Just like before, you can save big here by buying in bulk. Of course, if you use a more traditional size postcard, the cost is about half of that, but I like using the large size postcards because they stand out a lot more, and USPS has pretty strict requirements on what size you can send via EDDM. Ironically, in order to send via this very cheap method, you need a bigger-sized postcard.

Now if you want to really get costs down to

a bare minimum, you can do what I often do and actually print giant 8 ½ x 11 postcards at home. The trick is to get a printer like the Espon Eco Tank or the Canon Megatank. With one of those printers, you can print a two-sided, full-color flyer for about 5-8 cents, including the cost of the paper. While the initial investment is a bit steep ($250+), the printer has paid for itself probably 10x over in all the ink that I have saved. In total, the direct cost would then be just around 25 cents each, including shipping for sending these massive, double-sided, full-color flyers. So to send out 1000 of these monster flyers, you would only have to pay $250. Not too bad!

Besides the lower cost and bigger postcard, the other advantage of the EDDM program is that you don't have to individually address each postcard. You simply include a little graphic at the right-hand corner of every flyer and address it to "Local Postal Customer". You can still choose the neighborhood you want to send to, but you don't need to buy a list of addresses nor make a uniquely addressed flyer for each resident. All you need to do is print the same flyer 1000 times (or however many you want to send). This translates to massive time and costs savings.

The only downside with Every Door Direct is that you can't personalize each mailing. You'll need to write your copy and offer in a way that appeals to as many people in chosen postal route as possible. Choose routes that not only are in the geographical region you want to target but also in the appropriate age group, net worth, etc. By doing this, it helps to make up for the lack of personalization, which generally lowers conversion rates.

With targeting and cost problem fairly mitigated, the final problem is tracking. In the old days, you send out a marketing blast and hope for the best. Depending on the amount of post-sale interaction you have with your customers, you could theoretically ask if they were brought in from seeing a postcard, or follow-up from an email survey. For example, realtors can easily ask where people got the realtor's number from since they work face-to-face with their clients for a good amount of time. However, someone selling products on Amazon that is sending out postcards won't have that luxury, and so it would be better to ask via email.

In either event though, there are major limitations to the "Hope for the best" strategy. The biggest one is that even if you can track the sale source through asking or a survey, you won't be able to identify people who are interested in your product or service but not yet ready to take action (which, as we know, is about 80%). In many cases, the key problem is just this timing problem. They may want your window cleaning service, but their windows aren't yet dirty enough to warrant action. Without the ability to follow up and maintain that awareness, you could easily get beat out by someone else who hits the prospect with their marketing message once just before they actually read to make the decision to purchase - like when their windows are actually dirty. This means you either have to continually bombard everyone with marketing materials to stay top of mind or you have to figure out a way to identify the people who are interested in your product/service, but not yet ready to buy.

Since bombarding everyone isn't really an option unless you have deep pockets, the question is, how do you get people to identify themselves as interested, but not yet ready to buy with mail? There are two approaches you can take to this.

The first is complicated but results in a higher conversion rate. Essentially, what you do is offer some sort of freebie, but instead of asking for their email like we typically do on a landing page, give them a unique tracking code that is just for them to use to redeem the offer. If you have ever received a credit card offer with a pre-approval number, this is essentially the same thing. When the recipient enters the keycode in order to get the freebie/offer, it will then allow you to compare the keycode to your prospects list and see who exactly responded to your offer. If that sounds a little confusing, here's an example from personal experience.

Let's say that a Realtor is trying to drum up business by direct mailing a neighborhood. His initial offer is "Call now for your free home estimate." As we've established, most people aren't going to be selling their house this second, so they won't be calling for said home estimate. That's not to say they aren't interested in the home estimate; it's just that they aren't willing to pick up a phone to talk to a real estate agent to get it because they don't plan to sell for another couple of months.

Now let's say the Realtor changes it up and assigns individual tracking codes to each prospect. For example, the Smith's are going to be 1234. The Jones' are going to be 2468, etc. He then sends them a new marketing piece saying, "Get your free home valuation by typing in your keycode at BayHomes.com/value." Odds are many more people are likely to respond to this offer since they can take advantage of the offer anonymously and without needing to speak to a person on the phone.

Of course, the kicker is, right when they punch in that keycode, the Realtor knows who did it. If he sees the keycode being entered as 12345, he knows the Smith's responded. He can then send follow-up information over the course of the year to stay top of mind and even retarget them on Facebook. Again, not too bad for a cheap little postcard.

While this is the idealized version of the system since it allows for the perception of anonymity and lowers the "transaction costs" by not requiring prospects to enter in their information, there is a much easier way of doing it.

The simplest way to do it is just to provide a link to the landing page that you are already using for your digital campaigns. For example, on the flyer you could advertise your bribe such as you do in your online ads, and then provide said link to your landing page where they can download your bribe. The prospects will then just enter their email and then instantly be added to your follow up system. No fancy codes needed. The only downside is you won't have their physical address like you would via the other method unless you directly ask for it.

To take tracking one step further, if you have analytics on your landing page, which I recommend you do, you can even see where the prospects are coming from as a method of tracking results. To install analytics, simply sign up for a free Google analytics account and paste a snippet of code on your site. Once this is done, Google will automatically start providing you with all sorts of useful information. Most importantly though, doing this will give you a good idea of how successful your campaign was relative to your other marketing channels. For example, you'd be able to see if you got 5 leads from Facebook, 17 from postcards, and 20 from Google, etc. Then based on how much you spent on each lead source, you could calculate the cost per lead and re-allocate marketing spend accordingly.

As you can see, by linking the direct mail piece to your website/bribe, it makes tracking results much easier. You can measure the response rate you get from the bribe and then track them through your marketing pipeline to see what kind of return you are getting.

Example: You send out 1000 postcards and get a 1/50 response rate (20 people respond). Of those, 1/20 will become customers, resulting in a $5000

LCV. If the marketing piece cost around $700, we are doing pretty good.

Quick Tip: One final tip I will leave you with is to have multiple calls to action. Have one for people ready to act now and the other for people who will be interested in the future. The act now call to action could be a time-sensitive coupon; the other could be a link to a freebie designed for the maybe later crowd.

Bonus Tip: For those who are "design challenged" like myself, Canva is an invaluable resource for creating incredible postcard designs and graphics.

Event Marketing

Let's continue exploring more offline methods and examine another far too underutilized marketing method - Events. Events allow you to both strengthen relationships with existing customers and build awareness with new potential customers. The power of events is in the fact that you have potential and existing customers right there, in person. No matter what type of business you are in, you can integrate event marketing into your marketing mix, often for incredible results. In fact, in my businesses, events have led to more business than any other type of marketing.

Types of Events

Naturally, there are many types of events to choose from. Some are more suited for some types of businesses than others, but some are business type agnostic. Literally any business can throw a party or hold an open house (not the for-sale kind). The trick is to determine what will be most cost-effective for the business and generate the highest returns. For example, a restaurant or pub could do very well by hosting a New Year's party, but a strictly online towel seller will likely not benefit dramatically in the awareness department from hosting a New Year's party (Though perhaps they could use it as a customer loyalty play, inviting their best customers).

The following are some general types of events and some examples of types of businesses that are likely to benefit most from said events.

Information Sessions: I personally love info sessions and have had great success with them. The people who attend these are usually very targeted, as they are already interested in your product or service. Moreover, it puts you as the authority on the subject. Because of those two factors, conversion rates are typically extremely high. They are cheap to host and the logistics are easy since the number of attendees is usually considerably smaller than just a general party. All it takes is a little food and a PowerPoint presentation. If customers are spread out geographically, making a live event challenging, this can be easily remedied by hosting a webinar, in which case, you don't even need food.

When deciding on the content, ask yourself

what problem your prospects are trying to solve or what overarching benefit do people hope to get by buying your product or service. For example, if you run a gym, you could offer an information session on the top 5 keys to weight loss.

In terms of presentation style, avoid hard selling your offering. You can definitely talk about it, but keep it light, informative, and engaging. High-pressure sales tactics are the best way to kill your event. However, it's perfectly acceptable to offer a discount for that day only to the attendees. This sly tactic puts pressure on them to decide but not in a way that damages your relationship. After all, you're the hero offering the discount. In the gym example, the owner could offer a free 30-day gym membership to attendees or a discounted rate if they decide to commit that day.

As in most things, follow up is key, and so you'll want to find a way to get contact information from attendees. You could have people sign in, have people register online, or offer giveaways in which people will enthusiastically give away their contact information. My personal favorite of the latter is to host a raffle, which encourages people to give you their contact information and makes it fun at the same time.

It's also important to point out that while information sessions are great for awareness building, they aren't typically great for building customer loyalty. Assuming they already use your product or service, it should have theoretically solved their problem already, unless your product/service is just one tool in the arsenal used to combat their problem. Therefore, they aren't likely to be interested in the content of the presentation unless it is tailored toward existing customers as an upsell or you're teaching them how to use the product in a new way or sharing a new case study.

Parties: On the other hand, no event type is better suited as a customer loyalty play than a good party. On any given day, you can usually find some kind of excuse to host a celebration or party. If you run a restaurant, pub, or bar, you can not only build customer loyalty but also bring in new customers and even make a good amount of money in the process. Since you already have food, you simply need to bring in some entertainment and spread the word. For non-food-related businesses though, the costs will definitely be high since you have to bring in food, and unless you charge for the event, all revenue gained will be indirect.

However, if your business model can take advantage of a large number of untargeted people, then you can often make a party work to build awareness in a cost-effective way. For other types of businesses, it might be good to just have a smaller, client appreciation night, style of party. In terms of content, a thank-you-for-coming speech would likely be appropriate and you can include some business highlights in it as well; just be sure it doesn't turn into a sales pitch!

Launches: These are similar to parties, but

usually the people there will at least buy something from you. Back when the game Halo was huge, I remember going to GameStop with my cousin at 12 am to have some fun at their Halo launch party. We got the game, mingled with the other guests, and had a blast playing Halo while EDM music blast in the background.

Launches are typically used for physical products and are especially good for products that have some kind of hype around the launch. They serve to not only build additional awareness around the launch but also reward loyal fans for their support and employees for their hard work.

Scavenger Hunts: These are lower converting in general but are a good way to build long-term relationships. Additionally, the costs aren't too high and a large number of people usually participate. I once decided to test this marketing strategy and mailed 100 mysterious envelopes to random people in the area. By the end of the week, 20 people had participated. Of those 20, one eventually became a client. Not too bad!

Similarly, a sunglasses company tried this method. A participant would buy the sunglasses as the "entrance fee", then had to complete a bunch of challenges wearing the sunglasses and post picture proof to Instagram. It was pretty genius, as it even had the built-in virality due to the Instagram posts.

Scavenger hunts, much like parties, primarily benefit companies with general appeal. While some niche businesses could find success with scavenger hunts, without broad appeal, you'll likely end up with a lot of goodwill towards your company, but not a lot of sales which is why they work pretty good for apparel/accessories companies.

Community Cause/Charity Events: Feeling altruistic? Consider partnering with a charity and raise money through a silent auction or a crab feed. While direct business is limited, expect some decent PR as a result. Many times, blogs, newspapers or even a local TV station will mention the event (especially if you reach out and tell them about it). This can be fantastic and free exposure for your business.

Typically, bigger companies like to do these partnerships because they have already achieved mass awareness. Their goal has typically shifted to building goodwill and maintaining awareness, which these type of partnerships provide plenty of.

Paint Nights: Paints nights, in particular, are really picking up in popularity across the US. While an accounting firm is unlikely to host one of these, restaurants can certainly benefit from nights like these. They can not only make money from paint night directly but, with any luck, pick up some loyal customers too.

Competitions: Competitions are similarly great because businesses can actually profit from them directly as well as get their marketing message out there. They can charge admission for the contestants and can even charge admission for the viewers. Competitions are also likely to be picked up by media outlets, which gets your brand out there even more.

Competitions can be used in a variety of businesses. Own an apparel company? Host a design event. Sell video games? Host a gaming tournament. What's more, you can even record the events and upload them to YouTube for additional brand exposure. Hosting these certainly requires some creativity, but the results will make it well worth the effort.

Promoting Your Event

Once you've decided on your event idea and worked out the logistics, it's time to, you guessed it, start marketing the event. You might think it's odd to market your marketing event, but I assure you it is very necessary if you want the event to achieve a good level of success. After all, when is the last time you attended a party you never heard about?

To kick off your event promotion, go to your Facebook page and create the new event page. The reason I recommend using Facebook as your primary event platform is because whenever anyone RSVPs for an event, it will show up in their friends' news feed. This allows an event to go "viral" a lot more easily than a post. After publishing your event, anyone connected to your business page will be able to see it. However, you'll want to expand the event post's reach to be seen by more people that aren't familiar with your business. In order to do that, start up the ad creator as usual, but instead of traffic or conversion as the goal, choose engagement → Event Responses as the goal. After that, create the ad as usual, targeting your ideal customers.

After the ad is live, ask a couple of your friends to RSVP. Just like how no one wants to be the first to show up for a party, no one wants to be the first to RSVP. After that, you could consider sending out an email blast with the Facebook link to everyone in your database.

Feeling even more ambitious? Send out a postcard blast using Every Door Direct promoting the event and, again, have them RSVP through Facebook. Make sure, though, that the mailing is done in the same geographical area as the event or you'll notice a significant reduction in response rate. Even a few miles difference can have an impact.

DVD Mailers

Moving on from event marketing, I now want to share with you a brand new tactic that I think could be a game changer for many companies. I discovered it while running a real estate marketing campaign, but it has the potential to be used in a number of industries, particularly the ones that make significant revenue per customer.

The concept itself is rather straightforward; it is mailing informational DVDs to prospective clients. We can use these in a similar way to postcards, except these stand out far more, build more credibility, and engage with a prospect like a postcard never could.

If you recall from earlier, we talked a lot about how much more powerful video is compared with stale text. Well, imagine being able to leverage that video power to hit high qualified prospects like the ones on the Experian data lists and skyrocket your conversions.

After hearing the above, most people's initial reaction is, "Cool, but that must be really expensive". But here is the kicker, the tactic itself isn't necessarily a game changer; it's the price. For essentially the price of just **two** postcards ($1.50), you can mail a custom DVD in a self-contained mailer, shipping included.

Another great thing is that even if the recipients don't end up watching it, it's still pretty effective because, as mentioned, it's a self-contained mailer. That means you have four full-color panels on which to promote your product or service. At the very least then, it ends up being a fancy postcard for not that much more money. Realistically though, since DVDs are considered inherently valuable, many times people will keep them even if they don't watch them right away.

How you use the DVD mailer would really depend on your industry and price point. Higher price points definitely have the advantage since the DVD is a minuscule cost when compared to a $5000 sale. The other benefit is that since the sales point is so high, people genuinely want information before making a decision one way or the other. You can

Jumpstart Marketing

then provide that information and pitch your service at the same time since you'll be coming off as an authority.

As in all marketing strategies, this becomes more effective in the follow-up. They may not watch the DVD right when you mail it, but as long as you are following up with postcards, on Facebook, or via email, there is more chance they will watch it when the timing is right for them.

To give you a more concrete understanding of this tactic, let's walk through how my team used them for real estate marketing. We started out with a highly targeted mailing list of homeowners that were likely to be interested in selling their homes. Next, we wrote a list of topics that we thought they would be interested in. We eventually settled on an interview-style video where we discussed how to sell a house for the most amount of money. After some editing, we sent our final cut to a DVD mailing company along with our mailing list. The DVD mailing company then sent out this DVD, which we called "Sell for More!"

We then followed up with postcards every other month, offering to give them a free home valuation (the instant, online kind) that we discussed in the postcard section.

As we continued to mail them, they likely to remembered us as the ones who sent the DVD. Whether they watch it, give it to a friend, or even throw it away, it's all a win. Because even in the latter case, we are going to stand out in terms of credibility since we sent them a DVD literally called "Sell for More!" they'll probably think the agent we were promoting is worth talking to.

As you can tell, we use it as a cold open to build awareness, but it's also perfectly suited to be a bribe as we discussed before. In these latter cases, the overall costs would be cheaper as you would be sending out fewer DVDs in total to a more targeted group.

I always believe in learning from mistakes and I made two blunders when I first sent out a DVD mailer. The first was that I forgot to include a strong call to action in the initial DVD. I used a generic "Call us today..." call to action, which, as you know, I'm not a fan of. The far superior way to structure it would be the way we discussed doing the postcard marketing, which prompts prospects to go to our home valuation page that captures their contact info. Everything mentioned about the postcards holds true for the DVDs in that you can integrate it with your online efforts by having them take some action online. For example, at the end of the DVD, you could pitch your bribe and have them go online to get bonus material or whatever your bribe is. Once they take that action, you can add them to your list and retarget them exactly how we talked about in the postcard section. This kind of call to action is infinitely more powerful than the wimpy, call us today one I used.

The second mistake I made was using too much of our marketing budget on the initial DVD mailing and didn't leave enough for the follow-up part. From personal experience, the worst thing you can do is send out one mailing and never follow it up with anything else. The reality is, most conversions happen after seeing your content 6+ times. This makes it imperative that your marketing campaign is structured in a way that takes this into account. Instead of using an entire 12k annual budget on one huge mailing, split it up evenly at 1k per month and target the same recipients of the initial mailing. This approach typically results in higher conversion rates, but is far less sexy than one big marketing blast.

DVD Content Ideas

If you like the idea of sending out a DVD, the first thing to decide is how it will fit into your marketing strategy. You might use the DVD as a cold opener and follow up with postcards/emails to maintain awareness as discussed. Alternatively, you could use it as part of your follow-up system if a prospect shows interest in your offering. You could even send a DVD thanking all your new customers for supporting your business as part of a retention plan. After deciding on where it fits, you'll want to decide on the content of the DVD. Here are a couple of ideas to get you started:

DVD Content

"10 tips and tricks to..." Lists are highly watchable provided the information being presented is interesting. Let's say you are a travel agent; you could send a DVD out discussing the top 10 budget vacations for families and then pitch your services. Alternatively, you could send out something like top 10 mistakes families make when planning a vacation or top 10 ways to save money on your next vacation. In either case, the title catches attention and many people will end up watching it just out of curiosity. The key, of course, is to make sure the information will have wide appeal to your target audience.

Service Showcase: If a prospective client reaches out and requests more information, you could go above and beyond by sending an informational packet to the person, which educates, discusses your services, shares some information about you and your team, and even includes some testimonials.

Product showcase: Similar to the service showcase, consider a product showcase if your business involves physical products. Traditional catalogs are big, heavy, and expensive to make and ship. Why not showcase your top selling products on video? You could even do a product demonstration or create a theme-like Christmas gift ideas. At the very least, it's a lot cheaper than a catalog!

Local News/Events – For those in local businesses that simply require maintaining mindshare like Realtors or lawyers, sending out a quarterly

DVD covering local events/news/volunteer opportunities might not be a bad idea. They'll see your face and think, "Oh yes, it's Bob. Guess he's still alive. I should probably give him a call one of these days."

Infomailer – This is probably going to be the most common mailer. Basically, you're just going to provide information that your audience is going to find interesting. Typically, it will be in the "How to" form and is probably the same content that you would use for an info session. While it might not be as catching as "The top x ways to…", it should work all the same. Accountants could do one on how to save money on taxes or lawyers could do one on how to set up a living trust.

Hopefully, you've now got a couple of ideas that you can try out. You know best what your prospects are interested in learning since you probably get asked the same questions repeatedly.

Video Creation

After deciding on the content, it's time to create the video. While this intimidates many people, it doesn't have to. The only equipment you absolutely need is a good microphone, a video camera (a smartphone works), and a video editing software if you intend to edit yourself.

When I created marketing videos for my team, all I did was write up a basic script, set up the camera on a stool and started talking. It was nothing remotely fancy at all, but it looked and sounded ok. After that, I just popped it into my editor and edited out the parts where I messed up. If you are new to video editing, iMovie is the way to go if you have a Mac. It's very easy to use and makes the editing process a breeze. For editing on a PC, there are many options to choose from. I just use a cheap program called Filmora, but many higher-end solutions like Premier exist.

Once finished, just hop over to Upwork or Fiverr and hire someone to make the front and back graphics for the DVD case. It literally cost me $25. Finally, send in the graphics and your final cut to the disk maker of choice. I used Bison Disc, though, Discmakers is also pretty good. They can either directly mail them to your client list or send them in bulk to your home or office. From there, you would manually distribute them via in-person or by mail.

The great thing is, once you have it all set up, all it takes is a push of a button to reorder your marketing video. You don't have to re-shoot and edit every time. You have a very powerful, custom marketing weapon at your disposal whenever you need it.

One final tip I will leave you with is to make sure your audio is good. People will forgive bad video, bad editing, but not bad audio. The good news is, it just takes a $20 mic on Amazon to fix that. You can plug it right into your phone or video camera of choice, and you are all set.

JOINT MARKETING

Now you may have noticed a similar trend in our marketing tactics so far; they almost all require money! Obviously, some marketing methods cost more money than others, but almost all require some kind of financial outlay. Wouldn't it be nice if you could split the cost of marketing?

The good news is you can through joint marketing with another business. Essentially, you both put your marketing message on the same advertising piece and then split the cost of the campaign. You could then either pocket the extra savings or double the reach of your marketing campaign for the same price.

Let's use another real estate example since it's a pretty easy to follow. Realtors can theoretically target anyone since almost everyone buys a house, but oftentimes they specifically target homeowners to get listings. So who also targets homeowners? Lots of companies do: Mortgage brokers, financial advisors, landscapers, plumbers, accountants, title companies, insurance companies, etc. There is certainly no shortage of potential partners! All are targeting homeowners, and most importantly, none of them are in direct competition. This last part is key. It's important to identify the type of businesses that are similar in that you both target the same demographics, but not direct competitors to those businesses.

Once deciding who to partner with, the Realtor could then reach out and offer to do a mailing with the other partner, say a mortgage broker. Perhaps they would then mail out something like "Your Home Selling contact List" that includes the Realtor along with the mortgage brokers contact info along with some compelling call to action for both. By putting the contact info of both, the ad could theoretically be more valuable than just having one and, even better, the costs of the mailing would then be split.

Setting it Up

If something like the above interests you, the first thing to decide is who to partner with. Naturally, not all partners are created equal. I would recommend one or two core partners and create a lead sharing group with the rest, which we will talk about later. The reason I like this approach is because if too many companies get involved in something like a joint postcard campaign, your message would get lost in the noise. Imagine getting a flyer with five different companies advertising different things on it. It would be a mess! For this reason, usually just two is best, with the exception being if you are sending a "preferred contacts list" like the one in the real estate example.

When you begin searching for core partners, look for partners with fairly deep advertising pockets. You want your advertising spend to be the limiting factor, not the other way around!

Next, look for a partner who shares a similar trigger event. A trigger event we will define as an event that consistently spurs the purchase of two or more associated goods/services. For example, if someone is getting married (the event), they will need a venue, flowers, a photographer, etc. Any of these associated goods and services could launch a joint marketing campaign targeting people who are newly engaged.

Sometimes though, only companies that share the same trigger event are competitors. If someone's plumbing backs up (trigger event), they need a plumber and only a plumber. The only people that share that trigger event are the competitor plumbers. If that is the case in your business, then look to partner more broadly by advertising with those who share a common demographic like we discussed before.

However, think carefully before assuming there are no other non-competitor businesses that share a trigger event. Take restaurants, for example. At first thought, the trigger event is that a person is hungry; therefore, the only thing that can satisfy them is a business offering food (competitor). However, quite often, people make plans days in advance to go to a restaurant without being hungry at that very moment. Why? They are planning a night out. Typically, a night out will consist of food and some kind of entertainment, usually a movie. In this instance, a restaurant could partner with a local movie theater to send out a direct mail piece offering the "Ultimate Night Out" with a discount to the theater and the restaurant (or a free dessert or something).

Hopefully, now you've got a decent idea of who you might want to partner with. You can either focus on companies that share your trigger event or, more broadly, your targeted demographic. Often you'll get best conversions from the former since it tends to be a little more targeted. After deciding who you want to approach, the next thing to do is reach out and ask them if they'd be interested in doing a joint marketing campaign and split the cost. Depending on the company, you may not get them to split it 50/50, but if you have higher margins than they do (ceteris paribus), then it might be justified. If, on the other hand, they have higher margins, then politely bring that up and ask for at least 50/50.

During this meeting, they're probably going to ask you what you had in mind in terms of advertising mediums. Obviously, there are a lot to choose from, but you might consider direct mail as a place to start. The reason is that it's pretty easy to put both companies on a postcard. It's significantly harder to do, say, a joint Facebook advertising campaign. Some other ideas you could consider are events and billboards which are discussed next.

Events: Events work well because both companies can bring their customers together and share the associated costs. By working together, not only can they create a better event experience for all attendees given the combined event budgets, but the experience is much more likely to result in more business for both partners since each will be able to benefit from the others customer list.

Billboards: This cross-promotion strategy seems to be becoming more popular these days. A few weeks ago, I was driving through Concord when I saw a billboard for the Contra Costa County Sheriff's department. On it was a recruitment message followed by the logo of Bay Alarm in the corner of the billboard. I also have seen one from Apple advertising their iPhone followed by an AT&T logo.

In both cases, one company received a larger benefit from the advertising than the other which brings up one of the challenges of joint advertising. How do you determine messaging? Since you aren't in the exact same business, that can be tricky.

Naturally, if you share a similar trigger event, it becomes easier since it doesn't really matter whose messaging is on the card since one would refer the client to the other if the services are needed of the other company.

You then can either look for broader topics like finance or health and fitness, or you can take the billboard approach where one partner takes the lead and the other has their logo on it. In the former case, you might promote both companies under the finance category under the marketing message like "The two companies you can depend on for your financial future." It would then feature both companies and how they contribute the financial future of the individual reading the billboard. In the latter case, where one partner takes the lead on messaging, the messaging partner would contribute more given more prominence.

Lead Groups

Often times, you will know business owners who don't quite meet your criteria for a core partner but would be interested in working with you in some capacity. One great way to leverage these relationships for mutual benefit is to create a lead sharing group. In essence, a lead group just refers people to one another without directly advertising with them. If you are a plumber and you find someone who needs windows done, you would refer that person to the window guy in your group. Accordingly, if the window guy found someone who needed plumbing work, he would send you that lead.

Of all the types of partnerships, this is probably the easiest to set up. There are no approvals to worry about and no need to worry about finding messaging that suits you both. The major downside is that you are incurring the full cost of your promotions, just as your partner is. For this reason, a hybrid approach works well. Have one or two core partners to share advertising costs with and then form a lead group with the rest.

Affiliates

One alternative way of leveraging partnerships, which is used online to great success, is the affiliate marketing model. Affiliate marketing is about promoting someone else's product using whatever methods the product vendor allows in order to achieve some result, usually a sale. When the sale occurs as a direct result of an affiliate's marketing efforts, the vendor will give a cut of the proceeds to the affiliate.

This type of marketing is actually where my interest in marketing began. Essentially, I would promote other people's goods through video marketing and then get paid when I brought in a sale.

These setups are a win-win, both for the affiliate and the business owner. The affiliates benefit as they just need to worry about marketing your product or service, not actually supplying nor distributing it. The primary benefit for the business is all the free marketing upfront. Affiliates will spend their own money to advertise your product in hopes of selling your product. As a result, your product or service will start being promoted all over the web. Thanks to that, not only will your brand be more of an authority, but your Google search rank will likely increase as a result. As we discussed before, the more the people linking to you, the more people are "voting" for you to be higher in the search results.

Another benefit is that the company offering the program only has to pay for results, not effort. It's only when an affiliate **causes** a sale or brings in a lead, depending on the setup of the program, that the affiliate actually gets any money. For example, an affiliate could spend a million dollars promoting a product, but if no sales come about as a result, then the business owner doesn't pay anything (not even reimbursement for what the affiliate marketer spent on marketing).

The final major benefit is that you can generally see what kind of marketing campaigns are working by looking to see what your top affiliates are doing. Are they wording the benefits of your product or service in a way that you have not thought of? Perhaps, they are using an advertising medium like Facebook in a really interesting way to generate sales. It's not at all inappropriate to reach out, congratulate, and ask your top affiliates what they are doing that is working so well. This information is extremely valuable and can be used to launch a marketing campaign of your own.

Now before we discuss how to set up an affiliate program, some might wonder what the advantage or benefit an affiliate program has over a typical lead share group since a lead share group is free, whereas an affiliate program costs money when a sale is made.

While it may look like the programs are similar on the surface, the programs themselves are actually very different, and as a result, I recommend having both an affiliate program and a lead share group. We have already talked in length about lead share groups, so let's focus on what makes the affiliate program different, besides paying for leads or sales.

The first major difference is that you can partner with multiple people in the same industry, whereas you can't in a lead share. It's ok if you reach out to 20 accountants and ask them if they are interested in joining your affiliate program since you aren't promising to reciprocate leads with them, but rather offering money directly. As a result, it's totally ok to accept all twenty into your program. However, it's really not ok to have a lead sharing group with 20 accountants. You can't ask them to send you 100% of the potential referrals in exchange for just 5% of your referral opportunities! This is why I like the combo approach. Exchange leads with the top accounting firm and ask the rest if they are interested in joining your affiliate program.

The second difference is that affiliates don't even need to have a business in order for the affiliate arrangement to work. Essentially, anyone can be an affiliate depending on how you structure it. Your neighbor, your dog sitter, or even your crazy uncle Bob can all be affiliates and refer you business. Their business is sending you business.

Finally, unlike a lead sharing group that will only send you referrals as they run into them, affiliates will often go out of their way to get you results since they don't get paid until they get you results.

Setting up your Program

The biggest hurdle to setting up affiliate programs is that they are often a bit more challenging to set up than the aforementioned lead share group. First, you need to decide how you want to structure it. Should you pay per sale or by lead? How do you track where each sale came from?

In order to know what kind of program to set up, you'll want to consider what the most important metric for your business is. Are leads the most important thing or is it sales or perhaps, the number of people who accept your free trial? Whatever the metric is for your company, that should be the basis on which affiliates are paid.

After that is decided, you must decide how much to pay per result. If the result you are looking for is sales, will it be a percentage of the sale or a fixed dollar amount? For digital products, some companies offer affiliates as much as a 75% cut. For physical products, on the other hand, they might offer something as low as 5-10%.

Typically, for leads and other types of results like app downloads or pay per call schemes, affiliates are paid a fixed dollar amount. How much to offer is really up to you. It should be enough to entice people to go out of their way to market for you, but low enough to make sure the program will be profitable for you. The good news is, you can always raise or lower the amount depending on what makes sense to you. That said, typically 50% for digital products and 15% for physical products is a good start.

After that is decided, you'll want to decide how you will track the results of your affiliates. This is the trickiest part. Fortunately, if you are a local service business, for example, your tracking doesn't need to be high tech necessarily. If a prospective client calls and tells you crazy Uncle Bob sent them, then just cut the check to crazy Uncle Bob. Alternatively, Bob could call you up and say, "Hey, I've got a lead for you." You would then call that lead to make sure it's legit and then pay afterward.

For product-based local businesses, it is almost impossible to track affiliate sales offline. There is really no way of knowing if Bob referred Steve to buy that toothbrush he purchased on Tuesday evening. The best you can really do is ask them at the point of checkout if anyone referred them. But even in this case, the program will likely be more of a hassle than it's worth.

The good news is, if you sell products online, then tracking becomes the easiest of all. For online or hybrid businesses, you can give affiliates a special link that drops a cookie in the prospect's computer. This will tell you which affiliate is responsible for the sale, how much the sale was worth, and automatically pay them at a set period. While this might sound a bit complicated to set up, there are a variety of resources out there to help. Additionally, once it's set up, you don't need to spend any additional time on it. It's set and forget.

If you are selling a digital product like an ebook or educational course, you could use ClickBank to distribute your product. The main benefit of ClickBank is that there are a lot of affiliates that exclusively promote ClickBank products, so you can get a huge amount of marketing exposure from them. You don't even need to contact potential affiliates one by one; they simply come to you.

The other big upside is that you don't have to manage the affiliate program. You simply set the percentage or dollar amount you want to pay and ClickBank will handle the rest. You don't have to worry about tracking, paying or anything else. The downside is that you are limited to digital goods.

If, on the other hand, you sell physical products or services and you use something like WordPress to host your site (which I highly, highly recommend), there are a number of plugins that you can use to create a robust affiliate platform by syncing them up with your checkout page. One very popular one is AffiliateWP that integrates with WooCommerce. It will handle the majority of the heavy lifting for you and has great flexibility.

Alternatively, or in addition to, if you sell physical products on sites like Amazon or Best Buy, they have their own self-managed affiliate program already, so you can tap into their established network at no additional cost to you. For their programs, you literally don't have to do a thing.

Building your affiliate network

Like anything, building an affiliate network takes time. The key is to be proactive in building it rather than just setting it up and hoping someone stumbles upon it (unless you are using ClickBank).

After setting up the technical side of the program, you'll want to create an affiliate success kit that includes everything your affiliates will need to get going. This often includes ad banners, images of the products, articles promoting your product/service, and perhaps, even a recommended marketing strategy. Heck, you could give them a copy of this book!

Next, reach out to as many influencers or potential partners as you can and ask them if they'd be interested in joining your affiliate program. Tell them about the product or service, why it's awesome, and why they should promote your product ($$$). This strategy will ensure that you are bringing in more and more affiliates to promote your product as well as giving each and every one of them the best opportunity to succeed. And as we've established, when they succeed, you succeed.

Finding Affiliate Influencers

Online Businesses: For those with online businesses, focus on reaching out to bloggers or website owners in your niche. Additionally, you can target YouTube video creators or Facebook page owners that make content in your niche. You could even reach out to popular people on Instagram or Twitter. Many times, these "influencers" will just ask for cash up front for their promotional efforts.

If this is the case, many times, it's a blessing in disguise because often, the amount you would have paid out for affiliate sales would be significantly higher than what they are asking for in terms of upfront cash. However, the key is vet any influencer properly. Many so-called influencers are just posting for the enjoyment of fake followers, that is, they are as phony as their followers. When evaluating an influencer, go beyond the number of followers and look at post engagement. While this can be faked to, it's usually harder to game engagement. To be on the safe side, if there is any doubt in your mind, offer them an affiliate arrangement as opposed to one off cash payments.

Offline Businesses: For offline businesses, finding affiliates is even more straightforward. Get LinkedIn premium and then simply message all the business owners around you to see if they would be interested in joining the program. You could also put together your lead share system too in the same manner.

Putting it all together

At this point, we've covered a lot of topics and discussed a lot of marketing ideas and strategies. As I said at the beginning of the book, my biggest gripe with most marketing books is it that they give you all these great ideas and then leave you feeling overwhelmed, not knowing where to start. This causes people to start dabbling into the idea of the month without focus or consistency.

The following section is my attempt to remedy that by giving you a step-by-step action plan based on what we covered earlier. It should, of course, be tailored according to the needs of your business.

The foundational steps should come first in the order given, but for the others, the order isn't particularly important. In fact, I recommend that you do not do all the things in the plan, especially not at first. The best marketing plan is the one you stick with that gets you consistent results. For that reason, start rolling out your marketing plan slowly if you don't have a dedicated team. Pick a couple of awareness building ideas that you think will have the greatest impact on your business and start there. After a couple of months, evaluate how effective they have been and either double down on them or try out some new ideas based on the results you are seeing.

FOUNDATIONAL MARKETING ACTION PLAN

1. Create your website
    a. If creating a website yourself, then buy a domain and hosting from a site like GoDaddy.
    b. Install WordPress on the back-end of your hosting
    c. Buy a WordPress "theme" you like. Search (your industry) + WordPress theme. You'll find a lot of great ones to choose from.
    d. Install theme via WordPress
    e. Create a nice looking Home, About Us, Services/Products, and Contact Us page as well as any others that you'd like.
    f. Create your bribe
    g. (Optional but recommended) Create videos to post on your

about us and product pages.
2. Set up your Email Marketing System
   a. Decide what email marketing service company you'd like to use.
   b. Create a welcome email (The first email they receive after opting in for your bribe)
      i. It should include a link to your bribe.
      ii. If your bribe is digital, you can upload the bribe to Google drive, Dropbox, or even your own website if you aren't sure where to store it.
   c. Create your follow-up emails (Start with 8; create 8 emails to be sent in 8 weeks.)
      i. These will be the emails that are automatically sent out after the first welcome email.
      ii. Make sure they are informative, interesting, and subtly pitch your products or service.
   d. Schedule additional emails
      i. Start with one email every week or two so you don't get overwhelmed. You can manually send more out if you wish.

e. Create the bribe landing page
   i. Tell them why they should opt in to your email list to receive the bribe.
   ii. Make sure your landing page solution integrates with your email marketing provider.
f. Now integrate the email system/autoresponder to your website
   i. Usually, you just need to copy and paste a snippet of code that's provided by the email marketing company into your bribe pitch page. There are a lot of tutorials online and outsourcers for hire that can help if you get stuck.
   ii. Pat yourself on the back. You are done with your website!

3. Set up your Google page (if you have a physical place of business).
   a. Go to Google.com/business and claim your listing.
      i. Usually, just type in your business name and address to find it.
      ii. If it hasn't been added already, just create a new page
      iii. You'll then need to verify it

by either requesting a postcard or via phone depending on the situation.
  b. After verification, fill out the listing completely
     i. Post as many photos as you can
     ii. Fill out your hours
     iii. Post something with the new post feature
     iv. Insert in your website and phone number if you haven't yet.

4. Get Social- Choose the social media profiles you want to use. (Example is for Facebook and LinkedIn, but you can decide to use Instagram or Twitter.)
  a. Set up your Facebook Account.
     i. Go to Fiverr.com and buy a custom cover photo for $7.
        1. Make sure it includes the name of your company, contact information and other details on it.
     ii. Create a Facebook business page
        1. Fill out all the information on the page
        2. Upload the cover photo and your profile

picture, which is probably just your logo.
3. Invite all your friends to like the page.
4. Start scheduling some posts
    a. Decide on what type of topics you want to post about.
    b. Gather supporting assets like checklists, interesting articles, etc.
    c. Write some catchy headlines.
    d. Schedule the posts via something like Hootsuite
    e. If you don't want to deal with social media, consider hiring someone for it or outsourcing it to a company.

iii. Create your LinkedIn Profile
      1. Upload a good photo and fill out the profile completely
      2. Start connecting with your friends
      3. Decide who you want to target that you don't know
      4. Create a template you will use to reach out to prospects
      5. Send targeted a message using inMail

With that foundational stuff out of the way, we can now move on to awareness building marketing tactics. As I mentioned earlier, don't try to do too much at any given time. While it's certainly ok to try different things, don't try to do everything. Also keep in mind, you'll need to be consistent in using any given marketing tactic and patient for results. In some cases, you won't get any results for 6 months after implementing something, so don't get discouraged if you don't see immediate results.

Local Business Marketing Plan

This local business plan is going to be a mix of online and offline effectively and using many of the tactics we discussed earlier. The overall strategy, once set up, isn't very time-intensive. It runs almost on autopilot. This scalability is what makes it so powerful. The only downside of the strategy is that it relies heavily on paid marketing. Even with a core partner, costs are going to be high. For that reason, it is geared towards businesses that have high margins and high dollar amounts per sale.

1. Team Up
   a. Find a core partner to split the cost of marketing, particularly mailings.
   b. Start a lead group
      i. Get LinkedIn Premium and start reaching out to a number of reputable companies and ask if they are interested in forming a lead group.
   c. Create a very basic referral program.
      i. Decide how much a lead or sale is worth to you and create a referral program in line with those numbers.
      ii. Continue to reach out and ask businesses in similar industries if

they are interested in joining your affiliate program which very well may be just a set dollar amount per referral.
2. Find leads
    a. Decide what demographic you want to target.
    b. Purchase a mailing list from Experian that matches a particular demographic that you wish to target.
3. Create an Informational DVD
    a. Work with a core partner to create a DVD content that will appeal to the target demographic.
    b. Hire a graphic designer on upwork.com to create the artwork for the DVD.
    c. Have a DVD mailing company print and mail the DVD to the mailing list.
    d. Split the cost with the core partner.
4. Create follow-up postcards
    a. Design postcards
        i. Integrate postcards with your online bribe
        ii. Get approvals from

the core partner and split costs.
    b. Schedule postcards, perhaps one per month.
5. Facebook Ads
    a. Create a video ad
        i. Let the video ad target people interested in the type of product you are selling.
    b. Create banner ad
        i. Geographically target banner ad towards people who receive the postcard/DVD.
        ii. Offer bribe again or more information.
    c. Create a re-targeting ad
        i. Set the ad to target people who visited your website
        ii. Give a strong call to action in either a video or banner ad format.
6. Google Ad
    a. Determine the keywords your target customers are likely to use to find a business like yours.
    b. Create a Google ad targeting those keywords.

7. Plan some events
    a. Decide what type of events you want to organize and who you are targeting.
    b. Lay out a calendar and decide how many events you want to do and when.
    c. Create the event page on Facebook and then run an ad to promote it to the people you are targeting.
    d. Start working on the actual logistics of the event and decide how you want to capture attendees' info.
    7. Collect reviews
        a. Put together a list of all the review sites you wish to focus on.
        b. After the service has been provided or the product delivered, ask customers for a review and then send them the list with the review sites on it.

ONLINE PRODUCT SELLER SAMPLE STRATEGY

1. Get on Amazon or an e-commerce platform of your choice.
    a. List your product via Amazon seller central
    b. Send in your inventory
    c. Run an Amazon ad promoting it as a sponsored product
2. Start running Facebook Ads
    a. Just like in the other section, implement Facebook ads.
    b. If you just got started on Amazon, you might want to send traffic that way; otherwise, send it to your website's sales page.
3. Google Shopping Ads
    a. Follow the steps here https://www.google.com/retail/get-

started/ to create a Google Shopping ad that will target people interested in your products.

4. SEO
   a. Decide the keywords you want to target
   b. Optimize your website content around those keywords
   c. Reach out to big websites or blogs offering some kind of good content.
5. Build Reviews
   a. Same as before, but again, if you are short on Amazon reviews, start there.
6. Direct Mail
   a. Determine what demographic purchases your products and purchase a corresponding mailing list.
   b. Send a postcard or other marketing materials to get them to opt in for your freebie or go for the direct sale, depending on your price point.
7. Create an affiliate program
   a. If you have a Wordpress website, install the affiliate plugin of your choice.
   b. If you have a digital product list

       it on Clickbank
- c. Reach out to key influencers in your market and see if they are interested in being an affiliate or if they will promote your brand for a set amount of money.

Follow-Up Strategy

As we discussed already in length, having a good follow-up strategy is very important to the overall success of your marketing campaign. Here's a quick example of what your follow-up system might look like based on price point.

HIGH PRICE POINT

1. Create an informational Packet which will be used as part of the follow up program.
    a. Buy company-branded folders
    b. Print out some information about your company, your offering, and what makes you different from the competition.
    c. Write a short letter of introduction or handwritten note thanking them for requesting more information and explaining what is in the packet.
    d. (Optional) Bind all the papers together in a professional report
    e. (Optional) Include a credibility booster such as a book you've written or perhaps the DVD you sent out if they have not re-

    ceived it yet.
  f. Mail out the packet via USPS flat rate priority mail for easy and fast shipping as leads start rolling in.
2. Follow up with a phone call a week later asking if they got the packet
3. Send an email a week later. The content of the email will depend on if you were able to reach them or not.
4. A week later, send an email saying you are sending them a little something in the mail.
5. A week later, send them a small goodie via mail. It could be a gift card, a movie ticket, pen, etc. Just say you are sending it as a thank you for considering your service.
6. Send another email – again, content will vary.
7. Give them one more call.
8. Send a handwritten thank-you note, thanking them for their time and hoping that if they decide to move forward that they will think of your company.
9. After this, just send an automated monthly email. If they haven't shown any strong signs of interest yet, they're officially a cold lead, and you shouldn't waste your time on them anymore.

Low Price Point
1. Create your weeks 1-8 emails.
    a. They should vary between informative soft sells, hard sells, and testimonials of the product.
    b. Week 8 should be a discount as a last ditch effort to get them to convert.
    c. After the initial 8 weeks, set them up on the automated monthly email.
2. Use a Facebook re-targeting ad
    a. Target those who showed interest but did not buy by reminding them of the product via a Facebook ad.
    b. You can use an event to target those who added something to the cart but didn't buy.

LOYALTY PROGRAM/ CREDIBILITY BOOSTERS

Finally, here is our checklist for the loyalty program. While, perhaps, not the most necessary right off the bat, it's good to start thinking about it early.

1. Decide what type of loyalty program you want to run.
    a. Will it be based on visits, money spent, or something else?
    b. How can you make it fun?
2. Decide on the tracking format.
    a. Will it be tracked via an app on the phone? A punch card? Red envelopes to be given out?
    b. Again, how can you make it fun and engage the customer?

Hopefully, this book has given you a good starting point from which to jumpstart your marketing. No matter what direction you take, it'll require commitment to awareness building and dedication to the follow-up. Don't be like me in my early days of my marketing career, jumping from new idea to new idea without giving any idea the time needed to develop.

But with that said, do be creative. New marketing ideas should be experimented with. The key is to do it in a way that doesn't let it come at the cost of your previously established marketing campaigns that you know work.

Well, thanks again for reading. If you could drop me a review on Amazon, I would very much appreciate it! (And yes, this is part of my "building reviews" strategy.) If you would like to get in touch, shoot an email to Devin@jumpstartmarketing.org.

www.ingramcontent.com/pod-product-compliance
Lightning Source LLC
Chambersburg PA
CBHW021828170526
45157CB00007B/2721